Cooper-Wolfling

I0075209

THE SOCRATIC ECONOMIST
REFLECTIONS ON THE LIFE AND WRITINGS OF
ZANE SPINDLER

EDITED BY

XAVIER DE VANSSAY AND FILIP PALDA

Published by *Cooper-Wolfling*. None of the advisory board of *Cooper-Wolfling* are responsible for the opinions expressed in this text, which remain the responsibility of the authors and editors.

Editors: Filip Palda and Xavier de Vanssay
Typesetting and final design supervisor: Apnez de Rondfleur
Cover design and typesetting: Stare Zamecke Schody Studios. Set in Minion Pro. Pictures published with the permission of Xavier de Vanssay, Filip Palda, Craig Parsons, Roger Sandilands who retain their copyright to these pictures.

de Vanssay, Xavier, Palda, Filip–
The Socratic Economist / Xavier de Vanssay, Filip Palda.
Includes bibliographical references.
ISBN 978-0-9877880-6-1

About the editors

Xavier de Vanssay is professor of economics at Glendon College (York University) in Toronto.

Filip Palda is professor of economics at the École nationale d'administration publique in Gatineau.

Dedication

TO HENRY GEORGE (1839-1897), WITH WHOM ZANE IS NO DOUBT
ENGAGED IN AN EXTENDED DEBATE ON PROPERTY RIGHTS. WE RE-
GRET THAT COMMUNICATIONS ISSUES PREVENT OUR PUBLISHING
THEIR EXCHANGE.

CONTENTS

PREFACE

XAVIER DEVANSSAY AND FILIP PALDA

THE FRENCH SAY "UNE VIE d'analyse pour une heure de synthèse". A saying which Zane Spindler defied from the moment he crashed out of the gates of his Ph.D. program at Michigan State University in 1968 with a dissertation on the dynamics of *ad-valorem* taxation in hand. He started analyzing and synthesizing early in his life and kept up the pace to his death at the age of 68.

A quick glance at his list of publications gives the impression of a man with kaleidoscopic and possibly even chaotic interests. The constitutional basis of economic freedom, the relationship between human parasites and prey in the struggle for resources, the economics of squatting, the economics of war, the politics of regulation. The list of interests goes on. The number of papers published is daunting. What is remarkable is that Zane was able to maintain this rhythm of publication while being busily engaged on an international project of economic education. He divided his time between teaching in British Columbia and South Africa. He was also active in Japan and other countries of the Far East as a purveyor of public choice and also his own special brand of economics. Was it all a plan to spread his message? Yes and no are possible answers.

Zane had no plan and that was his plan. His approach to the truth was that you discovered it through asking questions or just posing the question "why?" He did not ask in a schoolmasterly way. That would have presumed some knowledge of the answer on his part. Zane was a Zen economist. The art of seeking without seeking. But despite his high-cheekbones and slanted eyes hinting of a Tatar and possibly Asian ancestry, Zane was anything but a passive truth receptacle. He was a Western intellectual down to his second-order conditions and that meant for him being a practitioner of the Socratic method. Such practitioners in economics are rare. Frank Knight of the University of Chicago was the epitome of this sort of economist. Zane was not a follower of Knight's but was one of his intellectual heirs in method.

And yet, it would be wrong to leave one with the impression of Zane as a scatter-brain academic. If one were to box Zane into providing one word that summarized his approach to economics, he would not like to give it up, but he would likely say "rent-seeking". So powerful was Zane's grasp of this concept, and so urgent was his need to educate those around him in its implications, that it could be seen as the *leitmotiv* of not just his intellectual life but of much of what he said and did. Rent-seeking logic touched all parts of Zane's life. Sometimes it made him appear a cynic, as when he equated under certain circumstances government and organized crime, or when he carried rent-seeking logic into the analysis of interpersonal relations. Was this really the well from which Zane drew inspiration? No doubt he would question our reasoning. That was in his nature.

Those who came under Zane's influence will have done so mostly without understanding what was happening. He was unassuming. This invited his interlocutor, whether a head-of-state or an undergraduate to send up a few ideas without fear they would be shot down. But eventually they did come down, with a bump. Because Zane had an easy way of making you question your ideas, and then would gently guide you to the self-destruct button where you would gladly atomize them in mid-flight.

He was no less demanding of his work. There is a two-foot stack somewhere, we are convinced, of research articles by him which Zane discarded because he believed they were not up to his exacting standards. Sort of like lost *Beatles* songs or a new satire by Juvenal waiting to be discovered in the Villa of the Papyri.

As well as intellectualizing, Zane was also very active on the public policy scene. Through his associations with several East-coast universities he helped advise government. He was one of the intellectual pillars of a budding think-tank called the Fraser Institute. He was instrumental in developing their economic freedom index in collaboration with Milton Friedman. He also instructed the Institute on how economics should be presented to the public and as such was in large part responsible for their remarkable success in the 1980s.

Zane however stepped back from public policy shenanigans in the 1990s to focus on the question of how countries attain and sustain economic freedom. Without such freedom the Malthusian cycle of constant poverty could never be cut. Zane saw, already in the 1990s, that the rise of a the predatory state foreshadowed a long descent into poverty for developed nations, as rent-seeking replaced wealth-creation. But he did not lament this development. Rather he saw it as an inevitable consequence of the remarkable 200-year explosion of personal wealth the West had enjoyed but which the West was busy destroying through misguided government policies of subsidy, taxation, and over-regulation. Zane though did not take umbrage at this development. He saw it as natural, and in the wider scheme of things, as productive.

How do you recognize such a man's achievements? Initially we thought of gathering his collected writings into a book, categorizing, and summarizing them. Copyrights would have raised the expense of such a project to prohibitive levels. And the result might not even have been instructive. Instead we opted to present Zane's accomplishments through several lenses. The second chapter of this book will no doubt seem eccentric. It is simply a list of his publications. The third chapter is a memorial essay by Zane's longtime friend and collaborator Cedric Nathan. While brief, this essay conveys the essence of the man and his opus. It also contains a brief photographic essay. The fourth chapter by *Simon Fraser University* economist Douglas Allen is a probing examination of Zane's ideas and his contribution to economics. The fifth chapter by Brian Dollery of the *University of New England* in Australia goes beyond the heartfelt to describe the details of Zane's life. In it we learn of Zane's almost mythical status to legions of admirer-follower-students. The sixth chapter gives us a glimpse of Zane in his own words, busy at his Socratic method in an extended exchange with Roger Sandilands of the *University of Strathclyde*. In these exchanges we see the subtlety of Zane's thinking and even though some of us come under his critical fire we cannot help but being grateful he bothered to think what we had to say was worth correcting. The seventh chapter shows Zane busy inspiring young minds and helping young colleagues advance their careers. It includes a poignant recollection from the Japanese economist Asahi Noguchi of *Senshu University* of his email exchanges with Zane, following a seminar. In a way, it is Zane's methodological testament. In particular, it shows the ideological intensity and depth of his understanding of public policy.

Throughout we have included some pictures of Zane.
CheerZ!

THE RESUMÉ

ZANE SPINDLER WAS A PROLIFIC academic. We were unable to include even a small fraction of his works in the present book due to the steep price publishers have put on reproductions of his work. In jest several us tried to calculate what it would cost to buy back the copyrights to his various writings. We stopped calculating after the sums rose into the high hundred thousands.

We toyed with the idea of categorizing and summarizing his ideas, but we ended up with the view that a presentation of his resumé was the fastest means by which to access his thinking. Zane took great care in choosing the titles of his papers. And he was devoted almost exclusively to the publication of academic articles. No books figure among his writings. Some will tell you this is the sign of a pure academic economist.

If you have access to a university computer then most of these articles should be freely accessible.

Zane Spindler's resumé

Personal: Origin: New London, Wisconsin, USA. Citizenship: Canadian; USA.

Degrees: Ph.D. & M.A. (*magna cum laude*) - Michigan State University. B.Sc. (*cum laude*) - University of Wisconsin.

Positions:

Tenured: Full Professor, Simon Fraser University.

Visiting: Professor, School of Business and Management, American University of Sharjah, 2007-2008.

Visiting: Professor, Seikei University, Tokyo, April-July 2005.

Professor, Yokohama National University, Yokohama, 2001-2002.

Professor, University of Cape Town, Various months,1988 - 2001.

Lecturer, Economics, University of Stellenbosch, Feb-April, 1991-1997.

MBA Lecturer, Business School, Univ. of Stellenbosch, Feb-April 1997.

MBA Lecturer, Helsinki School of Economics, Feb - March 1989.

MBA Lecturer, Graduate School of Business, UCT, Feb-Mar 1989,1998-9.

Reader, Economics, University of Adelaide, June-March 1985-1986.

Research Scholar, University of Paris, Sorbonne, February-March 1984.

Associate Professor, National University of Singapore, June 1981-82.

Research Scholar, University of Essex, October - June 1973-1974.

USAID Advisor, Colombia National Planning Dept., July-August 1972.

Assistant Professor, Michigan State University, Jan-June 1969.

Teaching:

Graduate: Public Choice (Ph.D., MA), Macroeconomics (Ph.D., MA & MBA), Managerial Economics (MBA), Business Ethics (MBA), Analysis of Economic Growth (MPE), Research Workshop (Ph.D., MA).

Undergraduate: Public Policy, Public Choice, Constitutional Political Economy, Law & Economics, Economics of Bureaucracy, Macroeconomics, Microeconomics, Public Finance, Managerial Economics, Money and Banking, Economic Dynamics, Macro & Micro Principles, Current Topics, Globalization.

PUBLICATIONS

2008   "Using Economic Freedom Indexes As Policy Indicators: An Intercontinental Example". With Xavier de Vanssay and Vincent Hildebrand, in *Public Organization Review.* 8: 195-214.

2007   "War as Rent-Seeking: A Public Choice Perspective
on the Pacific War". With Brian Dollery, in *Public
Organization Review*. 7: 21-40.

2006   "On Sharks and Seagulls: US versus EU Policy
Differences". With Xavier de Vanssay and Vincent
Hildebrand, in *New Economist*. May 16.

2005   "Alternative Monetary Systems and the Quest for
Stability: Can a Free Banking System Deliver in
South Africa?" With Maureen Bader and Adrian
Saville, in *The South African Journal of Economics*.
73: 674-693.

2005   "Constitutional Foundations of Economic Freedom:
A time-series cross-section analysis". With Xavier de
Vanssay and Vincent Hildebrand, in *Constitutional
Political Economy*. 16: 327-346.

2005   *"Is Central Banking the Best Monetary Regime for
South Africa"*. With Maureen Bader, in *The Free
Market Foundation*: Johannesburg, ZA, 64 pp.

2004   *"Nanshin:* Budget-Maximizing Behavior, the Imperial
Japanese Navy and the origins of the Pacific War".
With Brian Dollery and Craig Parsons, in *Public
Organization Review*. 4:135-155.

2004   "Does Money's Origin Matter? A Review of *The
State, the Market and the Euro: Chartalism versus
Metalism in the Theory of Money*". In the *Economic
Record*. 80: 260-61.

2004   "Monetary Regimes: A Public Choice Perspective". In *The South African Journal of Economics.* 72: 50-82.

2004   *The Deconstruction of Privatization.* FMF Monograph No. 37, The Free Market Foundation: Johannesburg, ZA, 38 pp.

2003   "How Do 'Parasites' Serve Their Host? A Graphical Analysis of Scalping". In the *Public Finance Review.* 31: 695-699.

2003   "Constitutional Design for a Rent Seeking Society: The Voting Rule Choice Revisited". With Xavier de Vanssay, in *Constitutional Political Economy.* 14: 95-105.

2002   "Privatisation as a Rent-Seeking Ideology". In *Economia.* 53: 31-42.

2002   "Constitutions and Economic Freedom: An International Comparison". With Xavier de Vanssay, in *The South African Journal of Economics.* (September) 70: 1135-1147.

2002   "The Public Choice of the Wealth of Nationals". In *Economia.* 53: 21-30.

2002   "The Laffer Curve". In Howard R. Vane and Brian Snowdon, eds. *An Encyclopaedia of Macroeconomics.* Edgar Elgar: 425-432.

2001   "Squatting as a Transition Problem in South Africa".

With Cedric Nathan, in *Economics of Transition*. 9: 557-573.

2001   "Public Choice versus Public Finance on The Social Costs of Capital Gains Tax". In *The South African Journal of Economics*. 69: 359-365.

2001   "The Political Economy of Capital Gains Taxation in South Africa: Part II The Public Choice of Capital Gains Taxation and Public Policy". In *The South African Journal of Economics and Management Science*. 4: 234-253.

2001   "The Political Economy of Capital Gains Taxation in South Africa: Part I The Public Finance of Capital Gains Taxation". In *The South African Journal of Economics and Management Science*. 4: 1-25.

2001   "Earmarking Not Tolling". *National Post*, March 8. Republished: Urban Renaissance Institute. http://www.urban-renaissance.org.

2000   "The Relevance of Constitutional Design: Rent seeking and Economic Freedom". With Xavier de Vanssay, in the *American Political Science Proceedings* 2000. http://PRO.harvard.edu.

2000   "The Public Choice of Cartels". With Xavier de Vanssay, in the *Journal of Public Finance and Public Choice*. 18: 3-22.

2000   "Unconventional Perspectives on the Political Economy of Capital Gains Taxation in South Africa". *Discussion Paper No. 45*, Applied Fiscal Research Centre, University of Cape Town, April.

1998   "Financing Aboriginal Title Settlements". In Roslyn Kunin, ed, *Prospering Together: The Economic Impact of the Aboriginal Title Settlements in BC*. (Laurier Institute: Vancouver).

1998   "Forward". In *Automobiles in Canada: A Reality Check*. Canadian Automobile Association. Digital Document: http://www.caa.ca/CAAInternet/onlinelibrary/autosincan.htm.

1996   "Constitutions, Institutions and Economic Convergence: An International Comparison". With Xavier de Vanssay, in the *Journal for Studies in Economics and Econometrics*. 20: 1-19.

1995   "The Public Choice of 'Superior' Sanctions". In *Public Choice*. 85: 205-226.

1994   "Is Tax Reform In the Public Interest: A Rent-Seeking Perspective?" With Xavier de Vanssay, in *Public Finance Quarterly*. 27: 3-21.

1994   "Freedom And Growth: Do Constitutions Matter?" With Xavier de Vanssay, in *Public Choice*. 78: 359-372.

1994   "Squatting as Rent-Seeking and Interest Group Competition: A South African Case Study". With Cedric Nathan, in *Urban Studies*. 30: 477-94. [Winner of the

Donald Robertson Memorial Prize as "most distinguished" *Urban Studies* article in 1993.]

1993   "Infrastructure, Privatization and the Rent-Seeking Cycle". In the *Journal of Public Finance and Public Choice.* 1: 19-27.

1992   "Prospecting for the 'Homework' Measures of Economic Freedom". With Joanna Miyake, in Steven Easton, ed, *Rating Economic Freedom IV*. Vancouver: The Fraser Institute.

1992   "Budgetary Imbalances". *Fraser Forum.* (January).

1991   "Measuring Economic Freedom". With Laurie Still, in *Economic Freedom: Towards a Theory of Measurement.* Vancouver: The Fraser Institute, 135-75.

1991   "Liberty and Development: Another Empirical Perspective". In *Public Choice.* 68: 197-210.

1991   "A Critique of the Spending Control Act". *Fraser Forum.* (January) 22-3.

1990   "South African Sanctions: Serving the Public or Special Interests?" With Herbert G. Grubel, in the *Journal of Economics and International Relations.* 3: 335-45.

1990   "Constitutional Design For A Rent-Seeking Society: Voting Rule Choice". In *Constitutional Political Economy.* 1: 73-82.

1990   "A Rent-seeking Perspective on Privatization". In *The North American Review of Economics and Finance.* 1: 87-103.

1990   "A Note On The Macroeconomics of Dis-invest-ment". In *The South African Journal of Economics.* 58: 98-103.

1989   "Regional Rent-Seeking in Canadian Sales Tax Reform". With Xavier de Vanssay, in the *Canadian Journal of Regional Economics.* 3: 367-380.

1989   "When the Property Market is Hot, the Property Tax Increases Are Not". *Fraser Forum.* (March) 28-30.

1989   "The Assessment Authority and the Assessment System". Submission to the Vancouver Municipal Tax Review Commission.

1988   "Canadian Tax Reform As Public Choice". With Michael Walker, in *Contemporary Policy Issues.* (October) 70-84.

1988   "Benefit-Induced Female Sole-Parenthood in Australia, 1973-85". With John McDonald, in *Australian Economic Papers.* 27: 1-19.

1988   "Work, Welfare and Taxation: A Review". In the *Canadian Journal of Economics.* 20: 81-684.

1987   "The Nationality of Exploitation versus the Exploitation of Nationality". *Fraser Forum.* (October) 8.

1985   "Rhetoric *vs.* Reality of Canadian Incomes Policies".
        In E. Arliz, *Current Economic and Financial Issues of
        North American and Caribbean Countries.* 333-41.

1984   "Bonus Pay Systems for Greater Economic Stability".
        With Herbert G. Grubel, in *Canadian Public Policy.*
        10: 185-92.

1984   "Italy: A 'Transfer Economy' in Crisis" and edited
        "Comments". In M Walker, ed., *Taxation: An Inter-
        national Perspective.* Vancouver: The Fraser Institute,
        345-49.

1982   "The Overstated Economy: Implications of Positive
        Public Economics for National Income Accounting".
        In *Public Choice.* 38: 181-196.

1982   "Political Economy of Regulation: A Review". In the
        Southern Economic Journal. 39: 300.

1981   "Balanced Demand and Supply-Side Policies". In the
        Journal of Economics Studies. 8: 3-21.

1980   "Oligopolistic Behaviour and the Theory of Repre-
        sentative Democracy". In *Public Choice* (Supplement).
        35: 17-27.

1980   "The Effect of Unemployment Compensation on the
        Rate of Unemployment in Great Britain". With Den-
        nis Maki. In John Edward King, ed., *Readings in
        Labour Economics.* Oxford: Oxford University Press,
        407-419 (Reprint of 1975 *OEP* article.)

1980   "The Allocative Effects of Wage-Price Controls: A Canada-U.S. Comparison". Ronald G. Wirick and D.D. Purvis, eds., *Issues in Canadian Public Policy*. Kingston, Ontario: Institute for Economic Research, 303-22.

1980   "Bricking-up Government Bureaus and Crown Corporations: An Economic Case for Privatisation". T. Ohashi, ed., *Privatisation: Theory and Practice*. Vancouver: The Fraser Institute, 153-79.

1979   "Towards a Theory of Aggregate Supply Management". With Geoffrey Newman, in the *International Review of Economics and Business*. 26: 1113-33.

1979   "On Budget Deficits as a Major Cause of Inflation". In *Public Finance Quarterly*. 7: 381-85.

1979   "More on the Effect of Unemployment Compensation on the Rate of Unemployment in Great Britain". With Dennis Maki, in *Oxford Economic Papers*. 31: 147-64.

1979   "Determinants of Canadian Social Assistance Participation Rates". With W.S. Gilbreath, in the *International Journal of Social Economics*. 6: 164-76.

1978   "The Right to Vote No: A Proposal for Revising the Voting System (and Resuscitating the F-Y Voter)". With Francisco Arcelus and Gary Mauser, in *Public Choice*. 33: 67-83.

1978   "The Unemployment Effect of Unemployment Compensation: An International Comparison". With Dennis Maki. In Herbert G. Grubel and Michael Walker, eds., *Unemployment Insurance: Global Evidence of its Effects on Unemployment*. Vancouver: The Fraser Institute, 339-58.

1977   "Rumblings about Jobless Benefits". With S. Christensen, in *The Canadian Banker*. (March-April) 18-19.

1976   "The Effect of Unemployment Compensation on the Rate of Unemployment in Great Britain". With Dennis Maki, in *Oxford Economic Papers*. 27: 440-54.

1976   "Endogenous Bargaining Power and Small Group Collective Choice". In *Public Choice*. 28: 67-78.

1976   "Insurance Induced Unemployment in Great Britain, 1948-1972". With Dennis Maki, in *Mercurio*. (June) 1-9.

1975   "Endogenous Bargaining Power in Bilateral Monopoly and Bilateral Exchange". In the *Canadian Journal of Economics*. 7: 463-74.

1975   "Universities Should Discriminate Toward Assistant Professors". In *Papers in Economic Criticism*. (May) 31-32.

1974   "A Simple Determinate Solution for Bilateral Monopoly". In the *Journal of Economic Studies*. 1: 55-64.

1974   "The Simple Economics of Crises". *The Canadian*

Banker. (May-June) 42-44.

1972   "A Prediction of the Effects of an Excise Tax Change on the Automobile Market". In the *Journal of Economics and Business* (Formerly *Economic and Business Bulletin*). 24: 66-68.

1972   "Deficits, Debt and Recent Stabilization Policy in Canada". *Canadian Perspective Series.* Toronto: Collier-Macmillan, 1-15.

1972   *Debt Management in Colombia.* Department of National Planning, Bogotá, Colombia, 66 pp.

1968   The Short-Run Impact of an *Ad-Valorem* Excise Tax on the Automobile Market: A Dynamic Approach. Ph.D. Dissertation, Michigan State University, 128 pp. Abstract: *Transportation Research* (December 1970).

CONFERENCE PAPERS, COMMENTS AND SEMINARS

2006   "Democracy and Economic Policy: Lessons for Asia?" *Asia-Pacific Economic Association Meetings*, Seattle, July 29-30.

2006   "On Sharks and Seagulls: US versus EU Policy Differences" (w/ X de Vanssay & V Hildebrand), *European Public Choice Society Meetings*, April 20-24; Scottish Economic Society Conference, April 24-26.

2005   "War as Rent Seeking: Some Public Choice Perspectives on Japan's War for Greater East Asia" Seminars on Interwar Macroeconomics Series, July 18, Sophia University, Tokyo.

2005   "Democracy and Economic Policy" Seminar at Seikei University, Tokyo, June 30.

2005   "Constitutional Foundations of Economic Freedom: A time-series cross-section analysis" (w/ X de Vanssay & V Hildebrand), *Symposium on Entrepreneurship, Innovation and Economic Development*, May 28, Feng Chia University, Taichung, Taiwan

2004   "A Public Choice Perspective on the Origins of the Pacific War" Seminar at the University of Stellenbosch, April 1; University of Cape Town, April 15.

2004   "Institutional Foundations of Economic Freedom: A time-series cross-section analysis" (w/ X de Vanssay & V Hildebrand), School of Economics Seminar Series, University of Cape Town, February 4.

2002   "A Public Choice Perspective on Common Currencies" Seminar at Yokohama National University, January 10.

2001   "The Evolution of Recent Land Contests in South Africa" (w/ C Nathan), Law and Economics II, *Western Economics Association International Meetings*, San Francisco, July 7.

2001   "Lies My Taxman Told Me: A Brief History of Dodgy Capital Gains Tax Rationales for South Africa" Seminar at the University of Cape Town, March 22.

2000   "Constitutions and Economic Freedom: An Interna-
       tional Comparison" (w/ X de Vanssay) , *World Eco-
       nomic Freedom Network Annual Conference*, Liechten-
       stein, November

2000   "Capital Gains Commentary" *Fraser Institute Sympo-
       sium on Capital Gains*, Vancouver, September 15, 2000.

2000   "The Relevance of Constitutional Design" (w/ X de
       Vanssay), *American Political Science Association Meet-
       ings*, Washington, DC, August.

2000   "The Relevance of Constitutional Design: Rent Seeking
       and Economic Freedom" (w/ X de Vanssay), *Western
       Economic Association International Meetings*, Vancou-
       ver, June-July.

2000   "The Public Choice of Common and Uncommon
       Currencies" *European Public Choice Society Meetings*,
       Siena, April.

1999   "Capital Gains Taxation Explored" *Fraser Institute
       Symposium on Capital Gains*, Vancouver, June 18, 1999

1999   "Privatisation as a Rent-Seeking Ideology" *European
       Public Choice Society Meetings*, Lisbon, April 7-9, 1999.

1998   "Privatisation as a Rent-Seeking Ideology" *Institu-
       tions in Transition Conference*, Bled, Slovenia, Sep-
       tember 24-26.

1997   "How Aboriginal Title Settlements are to be Financed: Commentary and Discussion" *Economic Impacts of Aboriginal Title Settlement Conference* Laurier Institute: Vancouver, November 15-17.

1996   "Constitutions, Institutions and Economic Convergence: An International Comparison" (w/ X de Vanssay), *European Public Choice Society Conference*, Israel, March 10-12.

1995   "The Public Choice of the Wealth of Nationals" *Pacific Rim Conference on Trade and Development*, Tokyo, 8/29-9/1.

1995   "The Year of Living Less Dangerously: An interdisciplinary Perspective on the New South Africa" Invited Seminar, Strathclyde Graduate School of Business, Glasgow, on the occasion of South Africa's Freedom Day, April 28.

1994   "Commentary on Constitutional Reform in SA". *Western Economic Association International*, July 2, Vancouver.

1994   "South African Games". *Western Economic Association International Meetings*, Vancouver, June/July.

1993   "Remarks on Measuring Economic Freedom" *Rating Economic Freedom VI*, Sonoma, CA, November.

1993   "Remarks on Coalition Theory" *Conference on Current Issues of the Pacific Rim*, Vancouver, July.

1993   "Commentary on South Africa's Industrial Policy" *International Western Economic Association*, Lake Tahoe, June.

1993   "Intergovernmental Fiscal Relations: Comments" *Canadian Economics Association Meetings*, Ottawa, June.

1993   "Constitutions, Institutions and Economic Convergence: An International Comparison" (w/ X de Vanssay), *European Public Choice Society Meetings*. Port Rush, April; University of Cape Town, April; University of Stellenbosch, April; *Canadian Economics Association Meetings*, Ottawa, June.

1992   "Do Institutions Create Efficiency or Does Efficiency Create Institutions?" *Mont Pelerin Society Meetings*, Vancouver, August-September.

1992   "Should Property Rights be Entrenched?" *Western Economic Association Meetings*. San Francisco, June-July.

1992   "Consociation Versus Unitary Government in the New South Africa" (w/ C Nathan), *Western Economic Association Meetings*, San Francisco, July.

1992   "Do Constitutions Matter? Implications for the European Social Charter" (w/ X de Vanssay), *The European Economic Association Meetings*, Dublin, August.

1992   "Do Constitutions Matter? Some Implications for Canada of Worldwide Experience" (w/ X de Vanssay),

The Canadian Economic Association Meetings, Charlottetown, PEI, June.

1992   "Freedom and Growth: Do Constitutions Matter?" (w/ X de Vanssay), *The European Public Choice Society Meetings*, Torino, April. Seminars: University of Hong Kong, Chinese University of Hong Kong, Nanyang Technical University, January/February; University of Cape Town, University of Stellenbosch, March.

1992   "Evaluating Economic Freedom" *Fifth Annual Economic Freedom Symposium*, Monterey, CA, February.

1992   "Canadian Sales Tax Reform," Seminar: East China University, Shanghai; National University of Singapore, Jan/Feb.

1991   "Comments on 'The Mercantilist Roots of Apartheid'" *Western Economic Association*, June/July.

1991   "Squatting as Spontaneous Privatisation and Redistribution in South Africa" (w/ C Nathan), *Western Economic Association Meetings*, Seattle, June/July. Seminars: University of Cape Town and University of Stellenbosch, April 1992, 30pp.

1991   "Is Tax Reform Really Worthwhile: A Rent-Seeking Perspective" (w/ X de Vanssay), *European Public Choice Society Meetings*, Dijon, April. Seminars: University of Stellenbosch, March; University of Cape Town, April.

1990   "Measuring Economic Freedom" (w/ J Miyake), *Economic Freedom Symposium*, Sea Ranch, California, November. Seminar: The University of Stellenbosch, April, 1991. 80pp.

1990   "The Public Choice of 'Superior' Sanctions" *Public Choice Society Meetings*, Tucson, March. 35pp. Seminar: University of Cape Town, April, 1991.

1990   "Regional Rent-Seeking in Canadian Sales Tax Reform" (w/ X de Vanssay), *The European Public Choice Society Meetings*, Konstanz, April. 20pp.

1990   "Constitutional Design for a Rent-Seeking Society" *The European Public Choice Society Meetings*, Konstanz, April.

1989   "Infrastructure, Privatisation, and the Rent-Seeking Cycle" *North American Economics and Finance Association Meetings*, Atlanta, December. Seminar: University of Cape Town, Oct.1990; University of Stellenbosch, Nov.1990.

1989   "Can Sanctions Be Welfare Improving?" Seminar: University of Natal, Durban, April; University of Cape Town, June; University of Stellenbosch, June; and Simon Fraser University, October. 30pp.

1988   "Rent-Seeking, Rent-Defending and Rent Dissipation" *Public Choice Society Meetings*, San Francisco, March. Seminar: University of Cape Town, August. 23pp.

1988   "Measuring Economic Freedom" *Economic Freedom Symposium II,* Vancouver, July, 29 pp.

1988   "Liberty and Development: Another Empirical Perspective" Seminars: University of Cape Town, September; University of Natal, Durban December; and Simon Fraser University, February, 1989.

1988   "Comments: Regulation and Electric Utility Customer Price Differentials" *Public Choice Society Meetings,* March, 3pp.

1988   "Comments on The Effect of Price Deregulation on the Competitive Behaviour of Retail Drug Firms" *Canadian Economic Association Meetings,* Windsor, June, 6 pp.

1988   "Comments on Corruption in Law Enforcement" *Public Choice Society Meetings,* San Francisco, March, 1 p.

1988   "Canadian Tax Reform as Public Choice" (w/ M Walker), *International Atlantic Economic Society Meetings,* Apr. 30 pp.

1988   "Comments on A Theory of Leadership and Deference in Constitutional Construction" *Public Choice Society Meetings,* San Francisco, March, 3pp.

1988   "A Rent-seeking Perspective on Privatisation" *North American Economics And Finance Association Meetings,* New York, December. Seminars: University of

Cape Town; University of Natal, Durban and Pieter-maritzburg, April, 1989.

1987   "Public Choice Aspects of Recent Canadian Tax Reform" (w/ M Walker), *Western Economic Association Meetings*, Vancouver, July, 35 pp.

1987   "Pension-Induced Single-Parenthood in Australia" *International Atlantic Economic Conference*, Munich, April, 21 pp.

1987   "Benefit-Induced Female Sole-Parenthood in Australia 1973-85" (w/ J McDonald), *Australian Economic Congress*, Surfer's Paradise, August, 26 pp. Seminar: University of Adelaide, September.

1985   "Balanced Budgets, Ricardian Equivalence and Interest Group Theory" (w/ J W Dean), *Public Choice Society Meetings*, New Orleans, February, 16 pp. Seminar: The University of Adelaide, August.

1985   "Comment: Federalism, Special Interests and the Exchange of Policies for Political Resources" *Public Choice Society Meetings*, New Orleans, Feb. 3pp.

1984   "Privatising the 'Law of the Sea': Comment" *Mont Pelerin Society Meetings*, Paris, March, 3 pp.

1984   "Privatisation of Central Banks" Monetary Seminar, Sorbonne, Paris, April.

1983   "Incomes Policies In A Rent Seeking Society - An Alternative Perspective on Recent Canadian Programs and Recommendations" *Symposium on Incomes Policies and Macroeconomic Management*, Singapore, March, 18 pp.

1983   "The Political Economy of Hope: Comment" *Mont Pelerin Society Meetings*, Vancouver, September, 5 pp.

1982   "The Market *vs.* the Non-Market Supply of Immorality" *Symposium on Morality and the Marketplace*, Vancouver, August, 10 pp.

1982   "Rhetoric *vs.* Reality of Canadian Incomes Policies" *North America Economic and Finance Association Meetings*, December 1982, 16 pp.

1981   "Some Lessons of Supply-Side Economics for Developing Countries" Central Bank of Ceylon, Colombo, and the National Institute for Public Finance and Fiscal Policy, New Delhi, October.

1980   "Italy: 'Transfer Economy' in Crisis" *International Symposium on Taxation*, Vancouver, September, 5 pp.

1980   "Fiscal Policy, Aggregate Supply and General Equilibrium" *International Atlantic Economic Society Conference*, Freeport, Feb. 30 pp.

1980   "Bureaucratic Supply, Public Good Prices and the Valuation of National Output" *Public Choice Society Meetings*, New Orleans, March, 15 pp.

1979   "The Allocative Effects of Wage-Price Controls: A Canada-U.S. Comparison" *Issues in Canadian Public Policy Conference*, Kingston, May, 17 pp.

1979   "More on the Effect of Unemployment Compensation on the Rate of Unemployment in Great Britain" (w/ D Maki), *International Atlantic Economic Society Meetings*, Salzburg, April, 38 pp.

1979   "A Superior Organizational Form for Public Good Production" *Public Choice Society Meetings*, April, 8 pp.

1978   "Oligopolistic Behaviour and the Theory of Representative Democracy" *Public Choice Society Meetings*, March, 20pp.

1978   "Crowding out of the Third Kind" *Western Economics Association Meetings*, June, 12 pp.

1977   "Towards a Theory of Aggregate Supply Management" (w/ G Newman), *Canadian Economic Association Meetings*, June, 55 pp.

1977   "The Determinants of Social Assistance: An Exploratory Study for Canadian Provinces 1968-75" (w/ W S Gilbreath), *Canadian Economic Association Meetings*, June, 27 pp.

1977   "The Determinants of Social Assistance in Canadian Provinces 1968-73" (w/ W S Gilbreath), *Public Choice Society Meetings*, New Orleans, Mar. 25 pp.

1976   "The Unemployment Effect of Unemployment Compensation: An International Comparison" (w/ D Maki), Vancouver Conference on Unemployment Insurance, September, 28 pp.

1976   "The Right to Vote No: A Proposal for Revising the Voting System (and Resuscitating the F-Y Voter)" (w/ F Arcelus & G Mauser), *Public Choice Society Meetings*, Roanoke, VI, April, 28 pp.

1976   "Aggregate Supply, Stabilization Policy and Achieving Macroeconomic Goals" (w/ G Newman), *International Atlantic Economic Society Meetings*, Washington, DC, Oct. 56 pp. Abstract: *Atlantic Economic Journal*.

1975   "Endogenous Bargaining Power and Small Group Collective Choice" *Western Economic Association Meetings*, June, 18 pp.

1974   "Columbian National Debt Management: Recent Trends and Future Improvements" Public Finance and Development Seminar Series, University of Strathclyde, Glasgow, March, 26 pp.

1974   "Administrative and Political Lessons of Controls: Comment" *Eastern Economic Association Meetings*, Albany, NY, October, 3 pp.

1973   "Debt Management Policy in Canada" *Canadian Economic Association Meetings*, Kingston, June, 32 pp.

1973   "A Regional Input-Output Model for Southern California: Comment" *Western Regional Science Association*, Monterey, February, 3 pp.

1972   "Evidence on the Effect of Debt Management on Aggregate Economic Activity" *Western Economic Association Meetings*, August, 18 pp.

1971   "Wage and Price Change Relationships in Post-war Canada: Comment" *Canadian Economic Association Meetings*, St. Johns, June, 7 pp.

1970   "The Structure of Asset Portfolios of Households: Comment" *Western Economic Association Meetings*, August , 2 pp.

1970   "New Automobiles as Superior Durables: Comment" *Western Economic Association Meetings,* August , 9 pp.

1969   "A Dynamic Analysis of the Effects of Excise Tax Changes on the Automobile Market" *Canadian Economic Association Meetings*, June, 40 pp.

1968   "Do We Need Measures to Moderate the Influence of Tight Money on the Mortgage Market? Comment" *Western Economic Association Meetings*, Eugene, OR, August, 8 pp.

IN MEMORIAM 3

BY CEDRIC D. NATHAN

ZANE AND I BECAME FRIENDS in 1988 during my sabbatical leave from the University of Cape Town, South Africa, to Simon Fraser University, British Columbia, where I taught a course on the political economy of South Africa. At that time, South Africa was the apartheid pariah state enduring the onslaught of international sanctions by the western world on the one hand, and a threatened invasion by communist Cuban troops from neighbouring Angola in the north, on the other. Contrary to expectations, the course was fully subscribed by interested students and faculty, who wanted to hear the other side of the story. Zane was enthused when I told him I was giving the course a public choice and constitutional economics emphasis, which, contrary to popular opinion, in many ways found sympathy for some of the apartheid policies. And so, as a public choice disciple, Zane and I became the best of friends. From now, he would pay annual visits to Cape Town over the next twenty years.

He gave public choice and the economics of government courses in the economics departments at the English speaking University of Cape Town (the oldest and most widely known university in South Africa), and the Afrikaans speaking University of Stellenbosch – Afrikaans originating from the original Dutch settlers at the Cape. Until then, there were no public choice courses at these institutions. He also gave courses at the business schools of both universities.

We established close ties with eminent visiting economists from Simon Fraser University (James W. Dean, Peter E. Kennedy, Herbert G. Grubel), and the University of Rochester (Ronald W. Jones), to name a few. Despite the lack of emphasis of public choice at the University of Cape Town, there was a strong free market tradition into which Zane fitted comfortably. In seminars and other academic debates, he was not shy, to engage and question the basis of policy arguments that may have dubious theoretical and empirical merit.

From the early 1990s, we internationalised South African economic debate by organising South Africa sessions annually at the *Western Economic Association* International annual conferences. The resulting appeal and support was unsurprising given the perceived miracle of a peaceful political transition from a minority democracy (white voters only) to a universal suffrage democracy (black and white voters from 1994).

In 1993 we published our prize-winning article in *Urban Studies*, on squatting in South Africa. This article explained a relatively new squatting phenomenon in South Africa from a rent-seeking, pressure-group perspective. At first sight, the invasion of private and public land by squatters appeared random. However, closer examination of the phenomenon revealed a perfectly rational set of responses to failure of government to define and enforce property rights. Having attended numerous meetings between competitive rent seeking interest groups, it became clear to us that there was something more systematic at work. Apartheid had been recently abolished (ANC unbanned in 1990). But the still whites-only government could no longer move people around the country to satisfy their own political goals. We gathered data in the form of reports of proceedings of meetings. These data appeared to fit the Gary Becker (1983) model of competitive pressure among lobby groups for political influence. The predictions of the article have come to pass that, unsurprisingly, the squatting episode expanded and defied resolution in the face of government policy failures. This aspect is developed in our subsequent article of 2001 (Squatting as a Transition Problem in South Africa, in *Economics of Transition*, 9 (3), 2001, 657-673).

The article, applies principles of transition to land tenure and squatting in South Africa. Political transition reassigned political property rights which produced contestable and rent-seeking incentives for squatting as a means to privatise land and redistribute wealth. Government failure to establish and protect private property rights in the squatter camp resulted in common-pool problems that resisted private and public resolution with consequent rent dissipation and social loss. In response to this retreat from duty, informal agents emerged to claim their own share of the prize. Without enforceable rules of capture, the growth of squatter camps in South Africa was predicted to continue. Subsequent empirical evidence has borne out this prediction. The population of the squatter camp has expanded from 2200 in 1991 to 20 000 in 2001.

South Africa had clearly become Zane's favourite country of choice. He was an ardent consumer of all the recreational pursuits Cape Town had to offer; a vibrant ballet and theatre programme, and awe inspiring views having climbed Table Mountain before breakfast, and Lions Head at full moon. Both of these are in line to become world heritage sites, and Table Mountain, one of the modern wonders of the world. Zane was always enthusiastic for lunches at enchanting wine farms twenty minutes drive out of Cape Town, accompanied by congenial companions. And, not to waste the grandeur of brilliant sun sets, he had acquired a west-facing beach front apartment for his retirement. Sadly, he was not destined to make use of it. He is sorely missed.

Picture gallery

ZANE WITH ISABELLA Villani, Tokyo, 2005.

FROM LEFT TO right Roger Sandilands, Craig Parsons, Zane Spindler after a successful ascent of Mount Fuji 2005.

FROM LEFT TO right Cris Lingle, Tony and Claire Snelgar, Roger and Liza Sandilands, and Zane, Singapore, December 1993.

ZANE AND XAVIER de Vanssay in Rochester NY.

Zane in his office at Simon Fraser University

Zane atop a mountaintop. The type of place where he thought and felt best.

Zane with Milton and Rose Friedman at the 1992 Monterey conference on economic freedom. Also in the picture is noted libertarian Walter Block in center with beard. At this conference Zane and Friedman, among others, hashed out what would become the basis for the measurement of economic freedom.

ACADEMIC FOR ALL SEASONS

4

DOUGLAS W. ALLEN

I MET ZANE SPINDLER FOR THE first time when Jimmy Carter was still President of the United States, inflation was eleven percent, Margaret Thatcher was elected Prime Minister of Britain, and the Village People had a hit song 'Y.M.C.A.'. Our first interactions came in the classroom where he taught me "Macroeconomic Principles." Knowing now, what I would only find out later, it is possible that he disliked teaching that class as much as I disliked taking it. It was a basic course on the Keynesian cross, a topic that never made much sense to me, and Zane's reserved style in the classroom, his meticulous (almost pedantic) use of algebra, and essay assignments all worked together to make me dread the course. Once finished, I made sure I steered away from him for the duration of my undergraduate studies.

About a decade later I was an assistant professor at Carleton University. When SFU asked me to move back west, my wife, who was not fond of Canada's capital, accepted the offer. Such is how, in the fall of 1990, I ended up with an office across the hall from Zane Spindler. Within days of my arriving, Zane started dropping by my office to chat. I was immediately struck by two things: he never wanted to talk about macroeconomics (much to my relief), and he shared exceptional insights with every conversation.

I knew from my earlier years at SFU that he was an avid squash player, and we soon started playing once or twice a week. Very quickly my first impression of a decade earlier was replaced with respect, and we began a deep and long friendship that only ended too soon with his passing in 2008.

In this brief little essay I want to touch on three aspects of my relationship with Zane: his academic work; his unique collegiate character; and some personal memories of friendship. In the current world of scholarship where so much is done electronically and often at a distance, a "Zane" like character is probably unlikely to arise in our department again. He came to work everyday, spoke face to face, was always aware of world events, and just made the SFU economics department a colorful place.

Zane the Scholar

I DO NOT want to go through a detailed accounting of all of Zane's work. Rather, let me give the briefest of surveys, and then focus on some of the key ideas in Zane's lifetime of research. Zane was a scholar throughout his life, and there was no time during which he was not writing or thinking — Zane was never deadwood. When he first began he was econometrically tooled up for the time, and he used this comparative advantage to study various aspects of taxation and unemployment. As time went on, Zane became increasingly convinced of the public choice approach to problems, and although he often wrote about specific problems, he was mostly concerned with big picture ideas related to constitutions, money, and the state.

With respect to his earliest work on unemployment (most done with Dennis Maki, and no doubt much done in conversation with Herb Grubel), it must be said that Zane was a leader in the idea that unemployment benefits can induce higher levels of unemployment. Together Dennis and Zane used the most sophisticated statistical methods available at the time to show that the British earning supplement increased the unemployment rate by 30% over a period of six years. Other similar studies would follow, and today this idea is common place and well accepted. However, at the time all three of these men were laughed at behind their backs for suggesting something so silly. Yet Zane continued on.

In 1988 he published a paper with a similar theme that showed high welfare benefits to single mothers could induce more single female headed households. This paper was also ignored for some time, before that idea became more accepted. Generally speaking Zane was not someone who saw a specific issue or puzzle, and then examined it. He was more interested in big, broad questions.

Still, there were exceptions, and these point to Zane's versatility as a scholar. The two papers of his that stand out in this regard are the ones on the Japanese Navy, and the other on squatting in Cape Town. Both of these papers no doubt stem from personal interest. Zane loved Japan: the countryside, the post-war accomplishments, the gardens, and the people. Zane also loved South Africa and Cape Town in particular. In both cases, his familiarity with the subject matter lends some authority to his writing.

With respect to the Japanese Navy, Zane points out the important struggles between the army and navy over budgets, and argues that the navies aggression against the U.S. was due in part to their attempts to capture larger shares of the revenue back home. With squatting, Zane and Cedric Nathan follow in some detail the various incentives of the players in zoning and land development in a section of Cape Town. This is a detailed, dynamic tale, that relentlessly exploits the public choice hypothesis. Indeed, the best way to read both of these papers is as detailed case studies of specific examples of rent seeking. The overriding theme of Zane's work was "Public Choice." He fully believed in the concept of rent seeking, and that in this idea one found answers to most of the grand puzzles and economic problems of life. He did not believe that any economic policy could succeed unless it took into account the different interests of the participants, the efforts to capture rents, and the secondary problems that result from this behavior.

As I look back over the papers Zane wrote, and recall the discussions we had about them, I'm struck by how broadly he saw the world through this lens. To him, Public Choice was not a hypothesis limited to elections and government budgets. Rather, it applied to everything. On this point, he and I often disagreed. In my opinion, a society always has an interest in curbing rent seeking behavior, and so in equilibrium I might expect it to be limited. Zane was not so optimistic. For him, rent seeking not only drove the design of many institutions to prevent it, but it also was at the heart of other institutions when societies failed to control it.

And so, Zane wrote about coalition formation, reelection, national accounting, sanctions, taxation, capital gains, constitutions, and money. Indeed, I think his 2004 paper on money regimes represents not only his best and clearest thinking. It also summarizes his life work. When he says 'Surplus dissipation could take many forms, but the ones of most interest to those who might hold or use common currencies, are the forms that impair a common currency's prospects for long term stability or even survival" (p. 54, 2004) he is really summarizing his entire approach to economics.

He was no Panglossian, and fully believed that rent seeking and surplus dissipation could exist as an equilibrium outcome for some time. As a result, he was always skeptical (perhaps even hostile) to any suggestion that public control necessarily implied some better allocation. Of course, he applied this thinking to the matter of a nation's money, and he was not one to support the idea of a world wide currency. In fact, Zane's concerns over the rent dissipation that could follow an imposed common currency foreshadowed many of the problems that were soon to follow with the Euro and the debt crises of Europe after the 2008 financial crisis.

On the lighter side, one cannot speak of Zane's writing without noting a few things. First, he loved big words and often one needs a dictionary on hand to get through his papers. He was "perspicacious," and he wasn't afraid to say so. Second, he loved quotes, and the funnier, the more distant from economics, and the more obtuse, the better. Most of his essays start with a quote and he loved to start every section with one. Finally, he liked to use graphs. For Zane, a graph was always worth a thousand words, and with some of his complicated graphs, perhaps he needed ten thousand words to explain them.

Zane the Colleague

IN MY OPINION, Zane's reputation and collegial role at SFU was the result of several factors. First, Zane began writing along public choice lines from the start of his career. During the late sixties and early seventies most economists were Keynesian on the macro side, and straight-laced neoclassicals on the micro side. The discipline was just beginning to spread its empirical wings, and concepts like rent seeking, transaction costs, information, contracts, and institutions were hardly in the vocabulary. In this environment, Zane never fitted into the mainstream. Second, the profession was, as it continues to be, mostly dominated by left wing, Gucci socialists, who like to use economics to rationalize their own tastes on how the world should be run. Zane was unabashedly a right winger, and he was skeptical of all government activity, even in situations where George Stigler would submit to state authority. Third, SFU never hired a second person in public choice over Zane's entire career, and although he had several friends who were kindred spirits, he never was able to muster a second vote on any type of theoretical or philosophical lines.

All of this made Zane a bit of an outcast within the economics department. He never had any influence on hiring, firing, or choice of seminar speakers. He was seldom consulted on matters of department policy, and was basically *persona non grata*.

Some, when treated this way, might become bitter, alienated, and drifters. Not Zane. Zane came to work every day, engaged actively with those who accepted him, and enjoyed tormenting others who ignored him. Zane had a delicious wit, and he knew exactly what to say or do to get under the skin of fellow colleagues who caused him grief. Of course, this never helped his cause. But one could tell from the little smirk on his face that he enjoyed saying outrageous things to get a reaction from his more politically correct colleagues.

Perhaps one example sheds light on this side of Zane. During the 1990s, the SFU campus came under a "reign of sexual harassment terror" as the university developed a misguided, and, as it turned out, illegal set of harassment guidelines. Among other notorious features the guidelines allowed complaints to be filed anonymously, and offenders could be "tried" without being informed. Some individuals decided to use this power to "dissipate surplus", as Zane might refer to it. Zane, always with a sense of humor, shot back in a uniquely Zane way. As all his friends knew, Zane was a consumer of art and was very familiar with the SFU art gallery and loan policy. On hearing about the new sexual harassment policy, he immediately went to the gallery and asked if he could display a particular piece in his office. It was a cartoon like painting of a woman in a dress from the waist down. The painting had a vertical section, but where it came to the ladies' ankle it shot out horizontally, and so the entire piece took the shape of an "L". Zane used the picture as a door stop in such a way that anyone walking past his office couldn't help but see it. Within days gossip started about how "offensive"this picture was, and the fact that it was placed in such a public space made it all the more offensive. It wasn't long before someone made the predictable anonymous harassment complaint. I still recall the smirk of enjoyment on Zane's face when he informed the SFU harassment office that he was merely displaying their own work of art! They quietly asked for it back.

That little episode describes my experience of Zane as a colleague. He was witty, not one to ignore his surroundings, and always full of good humor. Unfortunately, he was always too smart to become the victim of any practical joke. On many occasions I would send him fake letters from the university advising him that he would have to take some new courses to improve his teaching skills or that he had to rid his office of any abstract art work. On other times I would steal his keys (that he habitually left in the door lock), his favorite chair, or his gym strip, but every time he would just walk down to my office and give me a look to suggest I should grow up. Perhaps I just tried too often!

Zane the Friend

EVERY ACADEMIC RETIRES and dies eventually — otherwise how could the disciplines ever progress? But not every academic has papers collected and essays written in their honor.

I think Zane will be remembered most for being an incredible friend to those he was close to.

Part of his ability to be a friend was his willingness to be so personal. Zane was a bachelor most of his life, and he was very open about sharing his theories and experiences with women. He had theories about PMS control, on the role of protein in the female diet, and several theories of fertility and attraction of women. Of course, this annoyed most women ... at least the ones he was not interested in.

Consider the following example. On one occasion Zane was over to my house for a Sunday lunch. I had also invited my mother over who had recently been widowed. Zane and I were standing in the dining room, looking out the window when my mother drove in the yard. As I watched her drive in I glanced over at Zane who was also watching. A horrible thought crossed my mind, and I said to him in the sternest voice "don't even think about it." However, I quickly realized I had nothing to worry about. My mother and Zane were close to the same age, and one of Zane's theories was that the optimal age for a girlfriend was .5×(Age of Zane) + 7. Zane was about 64 at the time, so he really wasn't interested in anyone older than 39!

Zane was also a good friend because he was very giving. Many who knew Zane experienced his gift giving. Zane always remembered birthdays, and he always kept his eye out for particular presents that were appropriate. When he discovered that I was in favor of corporal punishment for children, he bought me a leather strap in the shape of a hand with "the encourager" embossed on it. When I showed it to my children, it frightened them so much it never needed using (the fact that they were all over 10 probably had more to do with it). When he discovered I liked roosters, he started buying me every odd rooster ornament he came across. When a secretary noted that she liked a certain style of shirt she saw in one of his pictures from South Africa, he brought one back for her on his next trip. That was the kind of person he was.

My own personal favorite story of his giving personality has to do with squash and Zane's obsession with cleanliness. Zane never trusted the gym to do laundry, and so he always brought fresh gym clothes to play squash in. Me, on the other hand, I never worried about a sweaty shirt and if it air dried in my locker for a semester that was fine with me. This drove Zane crazy. At one point he bought me a card for twenty washes in the gym laundry. Later he was horrified to find out that I was only using it once a month to "make the card last." Finally, he started buying me shorts and shirts under the theory that they might lengthen the amount of drying time between uses. Other people would have just refused to play me, but Zane's giving personality meant he had to find another way.

Zane was a good friend because he was so hospitable. In my thirty years as an academic there is no one else with whom I have shared so many dinner parties. A Zane dinner party was a special event. First, the guest list always included an eclectic assortment of people from all walks of life: artists, musicians, entrepreneurs, and other colorful types. I always felt I was there not as the token academic, but because of my farming background. What is a dinner party without a farm boy?

Second, the menu was exotic to the point of being completely foreign. Zane never admitted it, but he must have read cook books for a hobby. He could do things with mushrooms that were magic. Finally, the timing was relaxed and slow. Dinners may start at six, but nothing was every eaten before eight, and dessert seldom was presented until ten. Dinners with Zane were always an event, and they took place within his "art gallery-like" condo underneath enormous works done by local artists.

Finally, Zane was a great friend because he was forgiving. As mentioned, I met Zane in the fall of 1979. During my undergraduate days I spent a lot of time at the gym where I enjoyed squash, fencing, and weight training. Although I frequently saw Zane in the gym, I never said anything other than hello to him, and as far as I knew, he did not know me.

In this assumption, I was wrong.

Many years later, while Zane and I were walking across campus I happened to tell him that he was one of my professors. He was surprisingly silent and uninterested, and so I let the subject matter drop. The next day, he asked me why I'd brought the matter up, and I told him I was merely making conversation. As it turned out, on some occasion at the gym I went on some type of tirade regarding how much I disliked his class. As chance would have it, Zane was within earshot of those remarks. I think I hurt him deeply. When Zane told me of this I was ashamed, and apologized many times, but Zane would have nothing to do with it. He just wanted to drop it and move on.

For me, this says so much about Zane: he was forgiving. Had a student said the same of me, I would never speak to them again, and certainly would not seek them out as a friend and advocate for them. Zane died a young man. Physically he looked young, mostly because he took such good care of himself. Mentally, however, he was so active that his mind was also very young. And by today's standards, dying at 67 is young.

In speaking of death Zane claimed he wanted to live to 80 and then die suddenly. He got half of that right, and for an economist, batting 500 is pretty good.

References

Spindler, Zane (2004). "Public Choice Perspectives on Monetary Regimes". In *The South African Journal of Economics.* 72: 50-82.

MIND TRAVELLER 5

BRIAN DOLLERY

THE DEATH OF ZANE SPINDLER from pancreatic cancer on 30 December 2008 in Cape Town came as a blow not only to the economics profession in general, and more especially public choice economists, but also to Zane's legion of friends around the world. During an adventurous and colourful life, Zane managed the twin feat of making a valuable intellectual contribution to the economics discipline and simultaneously amassing a rich *potpourri* of friends drawn from an astonishing array of different cultures and language groups from around the world. It is a fitting tribute to Zane's qualities as a man and as a scholar that many of these friendships endured over decades and he remains sorely missed by those whose lives he touched. Zane had much to give and he gave it generously. In this chapter I shall try to capture at least something of Zane's work as a scholar of economics and his character as a man.

Life and times

ZANE A. SPINDLER was born in New London, Wisconsin in the United States on 2 September 1941. He graduated first from the University of Wisconsin with a Bachelor of Science (*cum laude*) and then went on to attend Michigan State University, where he graduated successively with an MA and a PhD in economics. His PhD dissertation was entitled *The Short-Run*

Impact of an Ad-Valorem Excise Tax on the Automobile Market: A Dynamic Approach.

Zane started at Simon Fraser University in Burnaby, British Columbia, as an instructor on 1 September 1967. He became Assistant Professor in June 1968 upon completion of all the requirements for his PhD degree. After a few short-term contracts he became Associate Professor with tenure in the fall of 1979 and Full Professor on 1 September 1990. In total, he served Simon Fraser University with great distinction for 41 years. Upon retirement, he accepted a position at the American University of Sharjah in Dubai. He was on a one-year leave period without pay from the American University of Sharjah when he passed away in late 2008.

A striking feature of Zane's career was his lifelong love of travel, often to foreign climes and exotic places. This is reflected in the host of visiting positions which Zane occupied over the course of his life. Beginning with a short stint as a USAID Advisor to the Colombian National Planning Department in July-August 1972, Zane embarked on an endless series of adventures abroad. He spent October-June 1973/74 as Research Scholar at the University of Essex in England, the year June 1981/82 as Associate Professor at the National University of Singapore, February-March 1984 as Research Scholar at the University of Paris in Sorbonne, the period June-March 1985/86 as Reader in Economics at the University of Adelaide in South Australia, and a six month spell in 2001/02 as a Visiting Foreign Professor in the Faculty of Economics at Yokohama National University in Japan.

However, his real love lay in the beautiful Western Cape of South Africa, especially the historic surrounds of Cape Town, Stellenbosch and the Cape winelands. Beginning with a stint in 1988 at the School of Economics at the University of Cape

Town in Rondebosch, Cape Town, Zane returned repeatedly to South Africa, holding numerous visiting positions at the University of Cape Town over the period 1988 to 2001. He also spent several spells as a Visiting Lecturer at the University of Stellenbosch, situated in the heart of the Cape winelands, not far from Cape Town, over the period 1991 to 1997. In addition, he bought an apartment in Cape Town directly below Table Mountain at the confluence of the Atlantic and Indian Oceans. It is thus perhaps fitting that Zane died in Cape Town with his wife Isabella at his side.

A glimpse of Zane

A 'GLIMPSE' OF Zane's colourful and intriguing nature can be garnered from the recollections of some of his longstanding friends, who kindly passed on their reminiscences to me. Several common themes emerge. A number of people fondly recall fine dinners at which Zane's culinary skills and exotic talents as a raconteur shone brightly. For instance, Professor Lindsay Meredith – a colleague at Simon Fraser University and friend of many decades – recounts his memories of Zane's dinner parties at his apartment in Vancouver and draws parallels with his thought processes:

> Zane was one of the only 'neat freaks' I have met who was as bad as me. The way he kept his house and his dinner parties was a good indicator of how he thought as well. Everything was beautifully organized with no mess or confusion. Yes he washed up as he cooked. Zane's thought process worked much the same way. Well structured and organized. He kept to the issue until he was happy with the analysis. No random flights of fancy or discontinuities in his analysis. He built his arguments carefully to take him to the

conclusion he was trying to develop. He was a true gentleman. I miss him greatly.

Professor Doug Allen, another close friend and colleague at Simon Fraser University, also has affectionate memories of times past at dinner parties with Zane. Doug sent me the following recollection:

Ah, you put a smile on my face when you mention dinners! I recall several things about them. Firstly, you had to be in no hurry. There was no way you'd ever eat before 8 or 9 p.m. Secondly, the food was always amazing, always cooked only by Zane, never something you'd eaten before, and never, never, repeated. Thirdly, you always met other extraordinary people there, and they were never academics. Artists were often in the crowd, as often were former girlfriends. He always had good wine, and though I'm allergic, I would often drink too much and suffer for it. And finally, there was Zane pontificating some outrageous 'theory of something'. He was best when theorizing about women.

Doug recalls a couple of especially hilarious and risqué episodes of 'theorizing' on women, no doubt designed to evoke a reaction:

My wife, who adored Zane, got so mad at him one night when he started giving her advice on how to avoid PMS. It was hilarious. I too have exceedingly happy memories of past dinners in beautiful surroundings. For example, one warm and languid summer evening many years ago at a dinner party which included Professor Cedric 'Ceddars' Nathan (of the University of Cape Town), Professor Philip Black (of Stellenbosch University) and myself. We were roundly entertained by Zane in the splendour of a restaurant situated in an

enchanting winery on the outskirts of Stellenbosch, in the heart-
land of the Western Cape vineyards. Zane tested several wines at
length in deep discussion with the sommelier. They disagreed on
the vintage of a given glass of wine. The sommelier disappeared,
returning with the manager, who - after a great show of sniffing
and tasting – and to the hilarity of all, declared in favour of Zane's
diagnosis!

On another wonderful occasion, attended by *inter alia*
Professor Ronald Jones (of the University of Rochester),
Professor Herbert Grubel (of Simon Fraser University and
a Reform Party Member of the Canadian Parliament), and
Paul Currie (then a serving New South Wales Police Officer
and a lifelong carnivore), I recall Zane serving an exotic salad
together with Israeli wine for dinner. My contribution to the
collective peace consisted of sternly tapping Paul's leg under
the table to restrain him from his customary declaimer that
anything other than meat was 'food that food eats'! Apart from
his gastronomic exertions that evening, Zane played an exem-
plary role in overseeing a fascinating debate between Ron and
Herb on the evolution of modern economics.

A second common theme revolves around Zane's penchant
for fast and fancy sports scars. For instance, Professor Don
De Voretz, another colleague from Simon Fraser University
and friend of many decades, graciously sent me the following
recollection:

I had the good fortune to know Zane for 40 years and enjoy the
benefits of many of his nominally bad investment decisions. In
particular, I remember in the late 1970s when Zane decided that
an expensive Italian car would be a good investment for him. He
proceeded to purchase a Ferrari or some such thing and found that

he no longer had use for his excellent Fiat Sport Spider. As a recent bachelor Zane offered the Spider at well below market value to me to enhance my sex life. At that point I began to understand the type of return Zane sought with his more exotic investments in houses, art and cars. Oh how foolish we economists were to deride him by assessing his purchases on strict economic grounds. Oh yes, he took the Fiat for a last spin and filled the gas tank for me!

Dr. Lindsay Meredith has analogous recollections of Zane's love affair with speed and automobiles:

He liked fast cars and liked to drive them that way. I remember once he ran a yellow light and a motorcycle cop immediately pulled us over. The cop said: 'You ran a yellow light'. Zane said: 'I was too close to the intersection to be able to stop safely'. The cop said: 'If you would #@$%^&* slow down you'd have more than enough time to stop'. That was one of our luckier interactions. The cop let him go. Suffice it to say Zane had one of the largest collections of radar detectors I have ever seen.

Almost all of Zane's friends will recall the extraordinary, 'exotic' and often canny explanations Zane offered to explain observed phenomena. A particularly delightful example was kindly sent to me by Professor Filip Palda (of the École Nationale d'Administration Publique (ENAP) and the Fraser Institute and a close friend of Zane):

In early 1992, I was the senior economist at the Fraser Institute. I had been hired after the departure of Walter Block - note how I am careful to say I did not 'replace' Walter as you cannot replace something for which there is no substitute. Mike Walker decided to bring me down to Monterey to participate in the second or third round of discussions on how to structure an economic freedom index. Zane was there and on one of the tours of the historic marinas we broke away from the Walker-Becker-Friedman brains-trust and strolled by a tattoo parlor upon which Zane made one of his contrarian, but profound observations. To him tattoos were a highly rational economic act. They were a form of self-mutilation undertaken by individuals who desperately sought membership in a social subclass. The price of membership to this class was the pain and expense of mutilating yourself. The form of the tattoo was a brand that identified you and qualified you for the benefits of membership. To him, this was the very same economic act as the facial scars produced by ritualistic dueling between German undergraduates. These scars were entrance tickets to a club of upper-middle class functionaries and businessmen in Biskmarkian Germany. It sounds obvious, but then so do many profound truths you never think of until someone mentions them while strolling with you on an evening in Monterey. Yes, Zane was a very close friend for many years.

Professor Xavier de Vanssay of Glendon College (a doctoral graduate of Simon Fraser University and longstanding friend) recounts another exquisite tale which invokes the essence of Zane:

Before I left Vancouver to go to Toronto to begin my academic career in 1990, I asked my thesis director - the late Peter Kennedy - for some financial advice. He told me to 'observe what Zane did with his money and do the exact opposite'. Zane thus didn't have a great reputation with regard to financial affairs at Simon Fraser. However, one day Zane gave me a terrific comment on money that I will never forget and would like to share. He once was asked to teach a course on constitutional economics, as a Visiting Professor (at Stellenbosch University). The topic of his fee came up. He told the Dean: 'I don't value money very much'. So the Dean happily asked him 'if he should be paid a very small fee'. Zane replied: 'No. On the contrary, because I don't value money very much, it really means that I need a lot of it to compensate for my time'.

Professor Craig Parsons of Yokohama National University has provided an intriguing multi-faceted glimpse of Zane, whom he first met in Yokohama in 2001:

Zane was a visiting professor at my new home and university, Yokohama National University in Japan, in the fall of 2001. I believe it was Zane's first time in Japan, although as always the case with Zane, he was already quite well-read in Japanese history, cuisine and the like. I was only a couple years out of graduate school and so being able to chat with Zane on a nearly daily basis was great for me, opening my mind to other fields in economics, and indeed, other fields entirely. I was constantly learning from Zane, not only because of his seniority, but more because of his encyclopedic knowledge of just about everything.

In common with all of Zane's friends, Craig Parsons was especially struck by Zane's lifelong practice of extending *homo economicus* logic to almost all aspects of daily life:

While I live and breathe and see economics in everyday life now, at that time, I was mostly breathing textbook models and econometrics. It was thus a joy to see Zane making brief, clever observations about 'economics in everyday life'. For example, while waiting in line at the Yokohama National University cafeteria, a young student was fussing with his change at the cash register, causing a hold-up. Zane sighed a little bit and said: 'Oh well...the externalities of change (coinage)'. Similarly, on another occasion - at the same cafeteria - when I complained how inefficient it was that the lunch break between classes was only one hour, and the cafeteria, likewise was only open for roughly one hour, resulting in queues of nearly 30 minutes just to get in, Zane retorted: 'well, maybe it is efficient, if the cafeteria has a downward sloping supply curve'. In these and innumerable other instances, he was often the contrarian - as many of we economists are - but Zane would play this role sometimes for its intellectual attraction, sometimes for its shock value, but more often for both of those reasons at the same time!

Craig Parsons recalls a specific and particularly apt example of just this kind of conjecture:

> On another occasion, when we were strolling through the Yokohama campus - talking economics - I raised Milton Friedman's advocacy of a flat tax, with zero tax for those on very low incomes. In terms of this Friedmanite conception, while there are certain efficiencies, the tax regime nonetheless remains progressive in nature. Zane replied: 'Why not simply a tax on the poor instead?' Whether he was serious, or simply trying to expand my mind, was not entirely clear, but he certainly achieved the latter, time and time again.

Zane as a scholar

ZANE SPINDLER WAS formidable intellectual who produced well over 50 scholarly papers in economics and political economy over his career.

The wide-ranging and quintessentially inquisitive nature of Zane's mind is immediately apparent from a perusal of his publications, which explore topics as diverse as a 1975 piece presenting the case for discrimination in favour of assistant professors in *Papers in Economic Criticism* to an ingenious graphical analysis of the practice of ticket 'scalping' in the 2003 edition of *Public Finance Review*. Analogous geographic variety is unmistakable, ranging from an analysis of benefit-induced female sole parenthood in Australia in *Australian Economic Papers* in 1988 to an examination of the role of the economic motives of the Imperial Japanese Navy in the genesis of the war with Japan in *Public Organization Review* in 2004.

While a high degree of heterogeneity characterised Zane's scholarly work throughout his life, several dominant themes emerged. A common theme - which emerged fairly early in Zane's career - crystallised around the unintended and frequently unfortunate consequences of government intervention intended to promote various benevolent economic and social goals.

Papers in this vein include his 1980 investigation of the allocative effects of wage-price controls in Canada and the United States in *Issues in Canadian Public Policy*, a 1984 piece on the deleterious impact of transfers on the Italian economy in *Taxation: An International Perspective*, a 1990 article (with Herb Grubel) on the motives underlying economic and other sanctions against South Africa in the *Journal of Economics and International Relations*, a paper analysing infrastructure provision, privatization and rent-seeking in the 1994 *Journal of Public Finance and Public Choice*, a 1998 piece examining the funding of aboriginal land title settlements in *Prospering Together: The Economic Impact of the Aboriginal Title Settlements in BC*, and a two-part paper on the political economy of capital gains taxation in South Africa focusing on the public choice and public finance approaches respectively to a capital gains tax in *The South African Journal of Economics and Management Science*.

A dominant theme in his earlier work lay in the political economy of macroeconomic policy making, as perhaps best epitomised in his co-authored paper with Maki on the effects of unemployment compensation on the rate of unemployment in Britain in 1976 in *Oxford Economic Papers* and its successor (also with Maki) in the 1979 edition of the same journal entitled 'More on the effect of unemployment compensation on the rate of unemployment in Great Britain'. A good deal of this work concentrated on the unintended impact of unemployment assistance on stimulating the rate of unemployment. For instance, his chapter on the 'unemployment effect of unemployment compensation' in *Unemployment Insurance: Global Evidence of its Effects on Unemployment*, edited by Grubel and Walker (1978) explored this question.

However, after this early work, Zane Spindler found his intellectual home in public choice theory from almost its inception and he became a life-long contributor to this area, with a number of papers in leading public choice journals, including *Public Choice* itself, as well as frequent conference presentations at almost all of the various public choice associations across the world. Whereas some of this work concentrated on the advancement of the purely theoretical aspects of public choice theory, like his work on constitutional design in the 1990 *Constitutional Political Economy*, his 1994 paper on the relationship between constitutions, economic growth and freedom in *Public Choice* with Xavier de Vanssay, and his 2003 article on 'constitutional design for a rent-seeking society' in *Constitutional Political Economy* (with Xavier de Vanssay), a good deal of Zane's scholarship was devoted to the application of public choice theory to contemporary policy questions, such as his paper on monetary policy regimes in *The South African Journal of Economics* in 2004, his work with Cedric

Nathan on squatting in South Africa, and his papers with Craig Parsons and myself on the origins of the Pacific War in the *Public Organization Review.*

An important applied element in this work centred on the application of public choice theory to important questions in monetary theory. This line of inquiry is exemplified in his 2004 paper entitled 'Public choice perspectives on monetary regimes' in the *The South African Journal of Economics* and his prophetic article in the 2004 edition of the *Economic Record* on the origins of money and the Euro.

Notwithstanding the breadth of his work, it is easy to discern common philosophical threads. Foremost among these is the pivotal importance of individual freedom and its intimate relationship to economic prosperity and the open society. Zane also steadfastly followed a libertarian philosophical approach in his analysis of public policy in all its forms. While as a scholar Zane will chiefly be remembered for his valuable contribution to the literature on public choice theory, his readers cannot fail to be struck by his adherence to these guiding principles.

Concluding remarks

GIVEN HIS FULL and remarkable life, it is hardly surprising that Zane was quick to recognize kindred spirits who also revelled in travel and adventure in foreign lands. One such 'soul companion' was the British explorer, writer and soldier, Captain Sir Richard Francis Burton (1821 to 1890), a man famed for his accounts of exploration in Asia, Africa and the Americas at a time of high empire. On his Simon Fraser University website, Zane quoted at length from Burton's (1872, p.16) *Zanzibar: City, Island and Coast* which serves as a fitting epitaph to Zane Spindler himself: scholar, traveler and adventurer extraordinaire:

> One of the gladdest moments in human life, methinks, is the departure on a distant journey into unknown lands. Shaking off, with one mighty effort, the fetters of Habit, the leaden weight of Routine, the clock of many Cares, and the slavery of Home, one feels once more happy. The blood flows with the fast circulation of childhood. A journey, in fact, appeals to Imagination, to Memory, to Hope—the three sister Graces of our moral being.

References

With the exception of Burton, R. F. (1872), *Zanzibar: City, Island and Coast*, London: Trinity Brothers. all articles by Zane referred to here are listed in Chapter 2.

Thanks

BRIAN WOULD LIKE to thank Doug Allen, James Dean, Xavier de Vanssay, Don De Voretz, Herb Grubel, Lindsay Meredith, Cedric Nathan, Filip Palda, Craig Parsons, Nicolas Schmitt and Isabella Villani for their kind assistance. Brian would also like to acknowledge his sincere gratitude to Zane for encouraging him to visit Japan and thereby igniting a lifelong passion.

THROUGH THE RENT-SEEKING LOOKING GLASS

6

ROGER SANDILANDS

THE EARLIEST OF OUR EMAILS of which I still have copies date from December 1991. This was during the second of my stints (1990-94) as a visiting academic at the National University of Singapore. My first had been in 1982-84, and I owed this to Zane's recommendation while he was there in 1980-81.

He said it was "the nearest thing to Paradise in academia" and supported my application for a post. In December 1991, we were corresponding on his plans for a short return visit to see me and give two seminars: (i) Is Tax Reform in the Public Interest? A Rent-Seeking Perspective (with Xavier de Vanssay), and (ii) Freedom and Growth: Do Constitutions Matter? (also with de Vanssay). At this time Zane was also trying to persuade a colleague at Simon Fraser University to publish a review in the *Canadian Journal of Economics* of my recent biography, *Life and Political Economy of Lauchlin Currie* (Duke University Press, 1990). Currie had been a visiting professor at SFU, 1967-71, where he had been one of my teachers and a colleague of Zane's, and he later contracted both of us to do some consulting work for the Colombian government in Bogota where he was a top presidential adviser

Zane arrived in Singapore in January 1992 and in my diary I made extensive notes on our conversations during his two weeks there. These provide a good background to our subsequent email exchanges on property rights from perspectives based, respectively, on (i) my familiarity with the work of the nineteenth century American economist Henry George (1839-97), famous (or infamous) for his campaign for a "Single Tax" on land values, and (ii) Zane's familiarity with a very contrasting public choice theory on property rights and the nature of government and special interest "rent-seeking" that he had been teaching and writing on for many years.

As our discussions continued, Zane suggested that we use our emails as the basis for an article on the subject, perhaps with a title such as "Is the Georgian site-value rating proposal compatible with Tullockian rent-seeking?" or, more simply "Henry George meets Gordon Tullock". He was not worried about our stubborn failure to reach a meeting of minds. On the contrary he welcomed this. Shortly after, he surprised me by writing (in relation to Milton Friedman's statement that "the land tax is the least bad tax") that "I think we would probably agree on practical policy, but not the rationale. Anyway, today I am aghast at myself for asking you to take the pledge. If you did, who would be left to challenge in a discussion as a worthy opponent? E-mail is almost as good as having you here as a colleague!"

We never did write that joint paper, and I am delighted to have the opportunity to do that now, albeit sadly belatedly and as a heart-felt tribute to Zane's intellectual generosity and long friendship that survived our differences.

My selections focus mainly, but not exclusively, on property rights, and are chosen both to reveal our deadly seriousness in debate and also the playfulness that was part of Zane's warm and generous character.

But I begin with my diary notes on our face-to-face discussions in January – February 1992 that sparked so much of what followed.

Diary, Monday 27 January 1992

I WAS TRYING to find common ground with Zane today over "economic freedom", in terms of the Georgist prescription for limiting government participation to what it can raise through land value 'taxation' (or the charging of fees for exclusive use of land, according to its differential rent). Zane had great difficulty in swallowing the concept of surplus. Land only has value because of human effort and enterprise. I agreed, but tried to show why individuals do not significantly affect the value of any particular plot. That value is community-created.

He brought in the Milk Marketing Board to show that individuals with exceptional abilities would still pay 'over the odds' [read: win at auction] for a quota allocation. What he meant was that they pay a premium over all other bidders, for the quota – monopoly rent captured by the Board – but may still be able to make above-average 'profit' on their use of the farm and its quota. He didn't like the use of the term surplus, not, at least, with any pejorative or ethical connotation. If land-owners – or any other kind of monopolist – enjoy rents, that would just be a reflection of the price they or their ancestors had 'legitimately' paid, even if it were by force and fraud perhaps. Or, at least, when they incurred the necessary costs to persuade the legislature to grant them the privilege. If, later, others are prepared to bear the necessary costs to alter the constitution, maybe bribe the politicians to vote their way, then things could change. Till then, the costs clearly (*prima facie*) are not outweighed by the prospective benefits. QED.

However, he was made uncomfortable when I reminded him that if the state doesn't collect land rents they will have to collect some other type of revenue, *e.g.* taxes on wages, production, or other kinds of property (buildings, improvements, etc.) Nevertheless, he couldn't get over the objection, as he saw it, that a land tax, or fee, would drive people away from that area, and investment and effort would migrate to a place where the land tax did not exist. I think I eventually persuaded him of the fallacy of this line. But, in the meantime, he told me another interesting tale of the Vancouver harbour longshoremen who insisted on their exclusive right to handle all "split" containers. The work migrated to Seattle and the cargoes brought to Canada by rail and truck, until the Shipping Company successfully faced down a long strike, backed by new legislation banning secondary picketing.

First he said this showed that the Shipping Company's own actions restored Vancouver land values that had plummeted because of the migration of business to Seattle. Then he agreed the provincial legislature had something to do with it, so this cast doubt on his claim that any increase in land values were the rightful claim of the landowners alone. I showed him the diagram in my *JES* 1986 paper but he remained sceptical because the state isn't interested in charging the proper fee. The bureaucrats would rather give it to favoured 'clients' at a lower price, because its cost to the bureaucrats is zero. In private hands, however, the cost is not zero, and it would then go to its best use! I did not understand, he said, the economic interests of the bureaucracy. But the property tax (on land and improvements) operates more or less according to objective valuation principles (subject to zoning constraints, admittedly, and these are dictated by officials).

But he took my article away to read.

Diary, 28 January 1992

FURTHER DISCUSSION WITH Zane on rent. He seems to think there is no such thing as rent not created by individuals. He doesn't believe there is such a thing as a "community". If there are rents they will be sought and fought for. The fighter (physical, legislative, bribery) involves costs that will tend to the present discounted value of any expected future stream of "rents" which, to him, are just another kind of earning, with a tendency to be equated to any other earning, in terms of the going, 'competitive', return on expenditures of money and time (with its opportunity cost).

The planner's signature that changes the permitted use value of a piece of land – *e.g.*, Abbey Rose Garden [an English example] – from Green Belt to residential and shoves its value up by £1 million an acre has to be 'earned' (the time and effort involved in lobbying for the change, which will only be expended if and when the augmented land value becomes great enough to make it appear that the effort is worthwhile). Thus the successful individual who gains the windfall has not really obtained a windfall at all. By definition. *QED*.

He scribbled all over the margins of my paper on Henry George which, nonetheless, he claimed was 'excellent' (in bringing out the issues so clearly) – for him to shoot down more easily! He didn't have any faith in any government administering a rent tax (fee) system because the bureaucrats have no incentive to operate it, or operate it efficiently. Potential bidders in an auction system to determine the 'market' rent could just form a "distributional coalition" (Buchanan), or ring and sort out their share of the gain. (So he admits there is a gain?)

He's not convinced that one of the main keys to Singapore's success is the Land Acquisition Act, a crude but effective way for the state to capture a much bigger slice of economic rent than in most countries. He asks me to debate that with Augustine Tan [a colleague at NUS and an ex-MP], who has been aggrieved at having been expropriated at an 'unfair' price in the past. (Zane says this shows just how honest and even-handed the Singapore administration is here. Most unusual. He can't quite understand [prime minister] Lee Kuan Yew's motives!)

He says that if ever my proselytizing succeeds in getting LVT introduced, the question is then: how should the proceeds be spent? He thinks the money should (and would) go to those who have pressed for the change: me! Only then would my costs be covered. Only thus would I have been motivated to bother … There is absolutely no room for altruism in his view of the world.

Diary, 30 January 1992

ZANE INSISTS THAT land rents drive productive efforts and that Henry George failed to see its dynamic role.

He sees it as no different from a lottery. People buy tickets because they hope to be one of the lucky ones. But they can't all be lucky. In fact in the aggregate they dissipate all the rents because the value of the prizes is less than the total ticket cost. (The government then captures the 'profit'. How would he define that?) But no-one would 'invest' if there were no prospective prizes. Yes, but this is not productive activity! Likewise, buying land is not a productive activity. It is just a transfer payment.

But Zane sees rents not as transfer payments, because rent is part of GDP and GDP is production. This is to confuse attribution (incomes) with contribution (output's value). Just because rent must be part of cost in the aggregate, or, rather, for the individual, does not mean it has the same status as labour, entrepreneurship, capital and technology, or wages and interest. (Actually wages and interest do not necessarily reflect the contributions of labour and capital either, if Lauchlin is right.)

If there were no prospect of private individuals gaining any land rents, there would still be a drive to work hard, take risks, and invest in capital goods. For these yield wages, interest and also abnormal incomes if you have some special personal skill, or if you are the first to launch a new product or process. But those premia will be temporary. You only get the premia for special skills for as long as you apply those skills and/or until other people acquire these same talents. And an innovator can't keep the imitators out for long.

But contrast the owner of land. The lucky ones will find their plots are where a new railway station has been newly located; or oil is discovered (the discoverers are often not the owners of the land and so have to pay rents to those who are). These rents cannot be competed away by the creation of more land or more oil. (That's not quite true: if a hitherto unknown reserve of oil is discovered, oil prices may fall and the rents on existing wells may fall. But that's a special case, that maybe makes mineral resources – the supply of which is not known for sure – a bit different from bare land, the existence of which is known about – subject to details regarding soil properties and load-bearing capacities.)

Zane gives another example which he believes to be an appropriate analogy: he wrote a paper on rent-seeking that he has had trouble getting published, but recently saw something on the same subject in *Kyklos*. That undermined the 'rents' that Zane had hoped to get by being the first to get this idea published. He and many others are investing in this academic lottery. Some are lucky and gain rents. But many others have been hoping to get these rents and their combined costs (effort) have usually more than dissipated the total rents to be had. Yet it is the existence of the prize that is the motivating force. Take that away and you destroy the dynamic motor that drives the economic system.

(Cf. Allyn Young: "Profits are the 'reward of enterprise' where this means taking advantage of maladjustments, taking chances and acting on reasoned probabilities... More lose than gain but subjectively the majority anticipate great incomes. Socially, it is more important that 'prizes' be obtainable than obtained.")

My response to this is that this confuses true rent with the returns to risk and innovation. The latter gains are associated with individual effort and are relatively temporary. By contrast, if a piece of land suddenly becomes more valuable because of a decision to build a new railway station nearby, people cannot create or move land to that location to bid down its rent. And the rent can be something that continues to exist almost in perpetuity.

Admittedly, the owner always has a decision to make as to whether to hold the asset or sell it to invest in something else. If he invests in another piece of land he will pay a price that reflects what he expects its future earnings stream to be; and in fact land prices will be set by the market at a level that tends to equalize the expected return. But this would also be true if there were a 100% rent tax. In that case the 'sale' price of land would fall to zero but there would still be an active demand for land, for it is impossible to do anything without it. (A 100% tax on an increase in rent would keep existing land values at their existing level; in practice reformers might aim at a progressive increase in the rent tax, or fee, over a number of years, to obviate the hurt done to existing land owners, many of whom acquired land, rather than some other asset, quite recently.)

Instead, people would use their savings to invest in other, man-made, assets – houses, cars, factories, machinery, office blocks. They would also acquire title to land (space) on condition they pay the annual, market-determined fee for the privilege of exclusive use rights (subject to zoning restrictions, etc.). [Zane doesn't think the (free) market would determine these fees ...] The return on investments in man-made assets would tend to equalize. If investment in houses yielded a relatively high return it would be because prices were rising relatively rapidly, and this would induce more building activity. (With land, a rise in price does not call more of it forth. All that can happen is that the fixed supply gets used in different ways – a reallocative, transfer effect. This rationing function of price is necessary too; but with other things whose supply is elastic, price plays a role it does not play in the land market.)

Diary, 10 February 1992

"Is THE GEORGIAN site-value-rating proposal compatible with Tullockian rent-seeking?" Zane's proposed title (roughly) for a "discussion" between us. Zane insists that individuals do create (and destroy) rent. I agree they do in the aggregate, but that it is seldom the case that an individual has much effect on the value of a particular site.

There are exceptions: when a mega-project is master-minded by a single development corporation, buying a large tract at pre-development values and then selling later at post-development values where these include rents as well as the improvements themselves ... cf. American City Corporation, Maryland.

Diary, 11 February 1992

GAVE ZANE CH.11 of my book before he left. He left me a diskette with "a bit of a draft" on George. He asked if I had read George Gilder's *Wealth and Poverty*. I had not. Zane is impressed by how Henry George understood rent-seeking, but "had gone wrong" with his single-tax proposal. He was delighted to have his attention drawn to HG's "freedom is to wealth as sunshine is to grain". Re Gilder, see what he has to say about the entrepreneur. The entrepreneur differs from most of us in being more benevolent and less self-interested than most of us who are not entrepreneurial. They have to understand what motivates other people, and ensure they offer incentives to others. It may be enlightened self-interest, but it is nonetheless enlightened/ benevolent.

At this point Zane left for Vancouver (followed by a semester in Cape Town), and our discussions continued by email. Selections that concentrate on discussions relating to property rights follow. But, before leaving Singapore, Zane left me the following short draft introduction to an article he later hoped we would produce jointly but never did – till now – from our ensuing discussions. I responded to this draft in an email dated 14 February (with Zane's response on 17 February, as below).

Is a Georgian single tax possible in a Tullockian rent-seeking world?

THERE HAS RECENTLY been a revival of interest in Henry George and his economic ideas (Horton and Chisholm 1991; Sandilands 1986), and the applicability of his ideas to modern economic problems (Gray 1991; Backhaus and Krabbe

1991). Since George's Single Tax proposal was first put forward (George 1879), there has been considerable controversy over whether it was economically feasible – mainly in the sense of revenue adequacy (Cord 1985). However, there has been only scant attention paid to whether a single-tax regime is possible from a political economy perspective (an exception is Kochanowski 1991).

The Rent-Seeking Paradigm and the "Transitional Gains Trap" phenomenon introduced by Gordon Tullock (Tullock 1967 and Tullock 1980, respectively) implies that prospective rents tend to be dissipated by the competition for them, thus leaving no net surplus available for easy capture by a government's single tax. Further, there is not necessarily a net social gain from a government entering a rent-seeking competition in an attempt to capture rent on behalf of itself or its constituents. This latter result has been reiterated and clarified for the case of reform in general by Tollison and Wagner (1991) and for tax reform in specific by Spindler and de Vanssay (1991). This paper will extend and apply that analysis specifically to the single tax as a reform and as a target for reform. Zane Spindler, February 11, 1992

References

Backhaus, J. and J. J. Crabbe (1991) "Henry George's Contribution to Modern Environmental Policy: Part I, Theoretical Postulates." *American Journal of Economics and Sociology*. 50: 485-501.

George, H. (1879, 1981 ed.) *Progress and Poverty* New York: Robert Schalkenbach Foundation.

Gray, K.R. (1991) "Report on the Conference on the Social Collection of Rent in Eastern Europe and the USSR." *American Journal of Economics and Sociology.* 50: 148-156.

Horton, J. and T. Chisholm (1991) "The Political Economy of Henry George: Its Ethical and Social Foundations." *American Journal of Economics and Sociology.* 50: 375-384.

Kochanowski, P.S. (1991) "Site Value Taxation in a Declining City." *American Journal of Economics and Sociology.* 50: 45-58.

Sandilands, R.J. (1986) "Natural Law and the Political Economy of Henry George." *Journal of Economic Studies.* 13: 4-15.

Spindler, Z.A. and X. de Vanssay (1991) "Is Tax Reform in the Public Interest? A Rent-Seeking Perspective." (mimeo).

Tollison, R.D. and R.E. Wagner (1991) "Romance, Realism and Economic Reform." *Kyklos.* 44: 57-70.

Tullock, G. (1967) "The Welfare Costs of tariffs, Monopolies, and Theft." *Western Economic Journal.* 5: 224-232.

Tullock, G. (1980) "The Transitional Gains Trap." In J.M. Buchanan, R.D. Tollison and G. Tullock (eds.) *Toward a Theory of the Rent-Seeking Society* College Station: Texas A & M University Press.

[*Editors' note*: we have reproduced the references in the style supplied to us by Professor Sandilands]

Emails

Date: 17 Feb 92
From: Zane Spindler
Subject: TULLOCK

Hi, Thanks for your long message [of 14 February] which I am returning with comments. You wrote

> With reference to your introductory notes on whether a georgist reform is possible (desirable?) in a Tullockian rent-seeking world, you may be interested in a review of a 1989 book by Tullock, *The Economics of Special Privilege and Rent Seeking*, by John Bethune in the July 1991 *Southern Economic Journal*. There it seems that Tullock acknowledges that special interest groups can obtain unusually high returns on relatively small investments of bribes or political contributions, so that all the rents are not by any means dissipated. Why? One (of several) reason is that most people regard rent-seeking as immoral and therefore may choose not to engage in it. He also has an essay there that discusses tax reform and how it can be designed to reduce rent seeking.

I am familiar with this book – in fact, Tullock presented the lead article in it at a seminar at SFU in 1987. I wrote a paper in response which I presented at the Public Choice meetings the following year but until Tullock's book came out there was no obvious place to send.

One of my projects is to revise my paper now in view of the book and ship it to *Public Choice*. Anyway, I'll send you a copy and you can see the counter-argument which in part is that Tullock's observation was based on only viewing the tip of the iceberg.

You wrote

But there is a problem in defining rent-seeking. I think Tullock mainly has in mind things like persuading legislators to impose tariffs and quotas, which are obviously against the public interest. Even if the state were to auction the licences and so capture the rents for the state with a view, one hopes, to using the proceeds for "good" social purposes, this would still be a socially harmful move. By contrast, land rents are socially and economically important in allocating scarce natural resources as efficiently as possible. The question is only one of who gets them. It does not make sense to reduce them, unlike the case of rents from import quotas. Tullock apparently accepts that if rent seeking leads to moves that increase efficiency this is not rent-seeking by his definitions. I would claim that the land "tax" would increase efficiency, and would be a reform that would have social value. Particularly as it would permit a reduction of other taxes that have a harmful effect on incentives.

You must really read the Tollison/Wagner article I left you and think of what you said above in that context. Really, it is only because you have thought a lot about land rents and have read George that you think land is different; in fact, it is not different than any other input; in a greater sense all inputs are creation of man and their prices represent value-added (in the national income sense) and opportunity cost on the margin.
You wrote

You claim that the bureaucrats who collect the land rents would not have an incentive to charge the right fee or use the proceeds for social purposes. But surely the same kind of objection can be lodged against any of the existing sources of state revenues?

Exactly! That is why so few governments are run as economists think they should be! When are economists going to learn this very elementary object lesson? It seems so obvious and yet everyone seems to ignore it because it spells the death of the mainstream brand of public policy and, as psychologists note, the first stage in humans' acceptance of death is "the denial stage"! I hope you, at least, can skip this and all other stages to move on to "acceptance".

You wrote

> I think what I am saying is that it's OK for "the state" to seek rents from land, but not OK for individuals to do so. Individuals should be as free as possible to seek income from work, effort, risk-taking, their own special talents, etc., but only after first agreeing to pay to "the community" the market-determined value of the space they occupy in their daily lives, be it while they are working or playing or sleeping or making love, or whether there is on their space a house, a factory, a shop or an office or garden, always bearing in mind that the market value of the space will be affected by any legal or other restriction on the kind of activity or structure that may be placed on it.

The state is not an entity apart from individuals. It is composed of a subset of individuals but exists as an idea in the minds of some larger, minimal-legitimizing-subset of individuals. If wealth is not increased for this latter group by the activities of the former group, legitimacy will soon be lost and some of those in the state may lose their jobs or more. Note that neither of these subsets need encompass the entire population and hence the general interest. There is really a distributional question here which most non-economists would not be willing to hand over to some abstract state as you – and many others – apparently would. They would want to know whether they are likely to be in the redistributional coalition which would benefit from such a change. You (they) have not considered this explicitly because there is an implicit presumption that publicly employed economists will benefit from these policies. Well, it ain't necessarily so – as can easily be seen almost anywhere we choose to look (except perhaps, Singapore). Other distributional coalitions have often grabbed the lucre away from us.

You wrote

> To the extent that the proceeds are used to build roads, schools, museums or parks in the vicinity of your home or place of work, the value of your space will be enhanced or reduced – again as measured by the market, which professional valuation experts do know how to identify, more or less. Thus the benefit principle is admirably reflected in this arrangement. It would be genuine "reform". *QED*, truistically and all, I hope.

If you look what has happened nearly world-wide to government expenditure on the beneficial "infrastructure" you cite above you will see it declining relative to GNP and Budgets while transfers are increasing.

Date: 18 Feb 92

From: Roger Sandilands
Subject: LIBERTY AND JUSTICE, *QED*

Hoping to catch you before you leave…

Tollison & Wagner is near the top of my list of things to read, but meanwhile I remain unregenerate. Land is not a creation of man, only its value is. But the value of any particular site is not the result of the efforts of its particular owner, but of the collective efforts of present and past generations. Land captures value but it does not create it. If a fence had been put around a site at the corner of Trafalgar Square in 1900 and no-one had stepped on it for the last 92 years, would its current value be what it was in 1900? If not, why not? Because of the opportunity cost, yes; but not because of any real cost in creating that site. Just because something can command a price does not mean it has added value. Do not confuse attribution with contribution to GDP.

Cf. Allyn Young: "Nature furnishes free productive agents which, merely because no economy need be practised in our use of them, they are not productive in an economic sense. Thus in an economic sense the wind is not productive but windmills are. We harness natural forces so as to use them in production, but we attribute the product wholly to the harness." (Cited on p.358 of my book.)

Maybe this is not such an apt quotation because while we get wind free we do not get (intra-marginal) land free.

Anyhow, you can see I have a lot of denial left in me! Actually, I thought I had gone quite a long way in accepting the death of mainstream public policy. But I haven't gone nearly as far as your anarchist position. I accept there must be some government, with its servants, formulating and implementing policy on the appropriate sources of revenue and how to spend and redistribute. I just think natural resource rents (not rents from man-made restrictions such as tariffs and monopolies) should be the natural source of finance for infrastructure, etc. that enhances (creates) land rents, à la benefit principle; and that anything left over should be redistributed equally as a social dividend.

I came across another reference to your friend Jürgen Backhaus yesterday, in the latest issue of *Land and Liberty*:

Backhaus and Krabbe, "Incentive Taxation and the Environment", in Richard Noyes (ed.), *Now the Synthesis*, New York, Holmes and Meier, 1991. Also see R V Andelson (ed.), *Commons without Tragedy*, Barnes & Noble, 1991. Noyes' book is reviewed in *Contemporary Review*, Dec 1991. There it noted that last December (1990) Milton Friedman in The *Wall Street Journal* raised the importance of Henry George's philosophy. He once described the land tax as the "least bad tax".

I'm glad everyone was on good form at your anarchists' meeting. Another freedom fighter, Theodore Schultz, sent me a letter that I received yesterday in which he described my book as an intellectual gold mine, especially in regard to what I had to say about Allyn Young in the chapters you have not yet read.

Date: 18 Feb 92

From: Zane Spindler
Re: LIBERTY AND JUSTICE, *QED*

Roger, your 1900-1992 example neglects the real opportunity cost of holding land, which among other things includes the real interest cost from foregone alternative investments, real legal costs of defending the land against private and public incursions (perhaps by such people as the single taxers), etc.. In open competition by land developers this will tend to equal the price difference if correctly anticipated at each point where continuing to hold the land off the margin is determined.

No matter what my or anyone else's position or arguments we will continue to have governments; no matter what your arguments are, those goverments will continue by and large to be sub-optimal.

Congratulations on Schultz's complimentary remarks; unfortunately, JC [John Chant] has told me he has not revised his opinion [about carrying a review in the *Canadian Journal of Economics*].

Friedman has just published a new book entitled *Money Mischief* which has a section on how China was lost. You & LC [Lauchlin Currie] may be interested.

I will miss our dialogue at UCT. Somehow reading more in the newspaper about Winnie's [Winnie Mandela's] exploits will not compensate.

Date: 18 Feb 92

From: Zane Spindler
Re: LAND AND JUSTICE, *QED*

Hi! (Yes, I'm still here!) Just reread your message. The Young quote seems to be stating exactly my position. But I still agree with the Friedman quote. From a practical standpoint governments have to capture what they can.

However, user fees are my preferred choice and taxing land should be justified on those grounds (the benefit principle as you mention), not on the grounds that the state is the only legitimate rent-seeker (you may recall that governments espousing that line took quite a tumble recently and most have entirely disappeared – special interest groups, other than bureaucrats, simply would not put up with it – in the name of the general [rationally ignorant and rationally uninvolved] public). In short, Roger, I think we would probably agree on practical policy, but not the rationale.

Anyway, today I am aghast at myself for asking you to take the pledge. If you did, who would be left to challenge in a discussion as a worthy opponent? E-mail is almost as good as having you here as a colleague!

Congrats on the (possibly duplicate) publication. My Tax Reform paper was just rejected by the *JPE* (previously by *CATO*, *CPP*, and *Kyklos* in earlier versions). So next off to *Public Choice* where I have two other papers in the queue. Given the recent appearance of the T/W paper, I feel a bit more pressured to get it published somewhere instead of continuing to persist to make it available to the non-believers rather than the converted. However, it is probably too idiosyncratic and needs a general, simplifying rewrite. This is now a task for my co-author.

Date:4 June 92

From: Zane Spindler
Subject: Rents

Roger, I read the *AEA-P* articles and recommend the last two paragraphs of the last article. [The first article by Gaffney is a collection of mostly wishful thinking which he dignifies by the word "lemma", the "pros" and "cons" of which he adds up to determine no overall majority in favour of site-value taxation – what BS to be published in such a prominent outlet! The second article by Tideman has him tying himself up in knots – as Friedman aptly points out.]

I think the historic experiment set out by Friedman pretty well damns forever the idea that there is such a thing as site-value apart from human activity; to attempt to tax the "site-value" arising from such activity is to tax "labour", not land, and falls foul of the Lockean justification for ownership – thus constituting a "taking" (*i.e.* a theft) by the state or by those who currently "own" the state – if Henry VIII had attempted site-value taxation to enrich himself,

I am sure you would have condemned it; why should a similar move by those with current entitlements from the state receive any different condemnation? Are some thieves better than others?

Date: 4 June 92

From: Roger Sandilands
Subject: Henry George VIII

We don't yet have the *AER-P*. But I agree there is no LVT apart from human activity. The question is: does it all return to those who created it thereby? Or is it creamed off by landowners who – by dint of prior occupation by themselves or their ancestors, or through the transfer of land so occupied, or seized, and claimed as private property via sale of private titles – capture the rents that the "community" (a shorthand – I know you think there is no such thing) created?

The North American Indians got there before you did. Did they have a moral right to keep out all the newcomers except on their own terms?

Did the newcomers have the moral right, by virtue of superior arms? Might is right? Do the Amazonian Indians gathering today in Rio? (I saw a great film the other day about them: "At Play in the Fields of the Lord", with Tom Berenger and Daryl Hannah.) I can't remember the Lockean principle – something to do with taking only as much as you can use?

I am all for people keeping what arises from their own labour and man-made capital. But labour and capital generate more than their marginal product (APL>MPL) and the difference is a payment not to labour or capital – which are elastic in supply – but to pure scarcity, even if it be true that people do compete to get their grubby hands on this rent, dissipating much of it in the process.

But do you not agree that if taxes on labour and profits were reduced or eliminated while taxes on land rents were increased, there would be greater productivity and less "DUPE"? Henry VIII is not Henry George. Of course we need a democratic and enlightened government into whose hands to entrust the LVT revenues. I think the biggest theft is via taxes on wages and profits (and VAT etc), whereas LVT is not theft. That's my answer to your last question. I know it won't satisfy you and that I'm beleaguered.

From Fort Apache, Cheers, the Last Hurrah. Roger

Date:7 June 92

From: Zane Spindler
Subject: Marlboro/Henry VIII
Roger,

An interesting set of responses. My replies:

"The Good, The Bad, & The Ugly" from human activity is "creamed off" by everyone in the vicinity by simple virtue of their being there. Those who have some greater entitlement by virtue of some human created institution, such as private property rights or welfare benefits, get a specific – sometimes greater, on balance – share. These created entitlements sometimes enhance individuals' incentives to contribute to the common pie (of which they are allocated a specific share which may be greater, less or equal to their contribution) – as is generally the case for private property rights – and sometimes decrease individuals' incentives to contribute – as in the case of welfare benefits.

Much of what is created and valued exists only in the minds of individuals; some is passed through and valued by the market. If someone who hasn't contributed to the market value in some important way tries to capture a part or all of it – by theft, taxes, or (the non-market equivalent of taxes) regulation – the market value tends to evaporate, to move to the unmeasured or underground market /economy (studies of these economies show quite conclusively that their size is inversely related to the rate of tax/regulation/theft), to move "offshore", or to move back to the non-market (in the minds and hearts and homes). Gain-seeking, in its profit-seeking rather than rent-seeking form, establishes property rights to some of the proceeds from activities which are then run though markets generating market income for those holding such entitlements as well as for others who hold more general entitlements to the pecuniary result of supplying productive factors. Establishing such property rights is "productive" since it creates the incentive to undertake activity through the market which otherwise would be undertaken less efficiently outside the market or not undertaken at all.

Consider, for example, a song. Once it exists, it is clearly a PUBLIC GOOD (or bad if it is a rotten song!); it is neither exclusive nor exhaustive in consumption. Yet the public sector supplies us with very few songs – mostly, national anthems which probably constitute, on balance, public bads (especially if the opinion of those in other nations is given any credence!). Most songs are provided by the private sector – indeed many spectacular technological advances (music videos, CD's etc.) have been devised to allow those in private production of songs to better capture a larger share of the public good (value) created by the production of songs. Of course, private producers will never completely capture all rents, all net value, all producer/consumer surplus from the creation of songs. But the fact that they have improved their ability to capture part of it generally enhances the incentive to create songs of greater value. Suppose now that a government would try to capture 100% of the market value of the rent on any song once written. I think it is a safe bet that the "music industry" would retaliate, resulting in some compromise tax of less than 100% (retaliation using up real resources up to the value of the "rents" retained) or it would simply cease to exist and new songs would seldom be created again except by the "public spirited" song-writers. Clearly, here the government would be acting as a simple interloper or thief – its justification for claiming the right to take the "rents" (thereby destroying or downsizing the industry and the value it created) would be simply that it would have the monopoly on coercion which allowed it to do so – *i.e.*, might makes rights! If the government actually facilitated private production of songs by establishing copyright laws and enforcing them domestically and internationally, it could of course claim a share (but not all) of the loot without diminishing the quantity/quality of privately produced songs and indeed, within a certain range of public enforcement of private property rights, private output might be enhanced (the optimum here entails a comparison of enhanced private values versus higher taxes).

To return to the case of real property, the legitimate private way for any individual to get a share of the value she has created (or destroyed) by moving to an area is by buying a piece of real property (or by buying a share in a real estate cooperative or real estate trust which holds real estate in that locale – something every citizen [& sometimes even foreigners] can do if the government allows private ownership of property [in Singapore one's share comes from holding shares of CPF]). Generally, one's ability to create value in a locale is related to the human and non-human capital one brings to it, as is one's ability to buy property there [hence, one's ability to capture is generally in rough proportion to one's ability to create]. [One can also capture one's share of uncompensated (by wage or price) value one creates in working for or buying from a corporation by buying its shares (even the poorest worker/consumer can usually afford at least one share which allows the capture of about the amount of excess value they may have contributed).]

The legitimate way for governments to get their share of the value they create by wise public investment in infrastructure and by wise and frugal administration is to realize the value of crown lands held within the locale and by user fees in the form of a low rate levy on property values within the locale – that is, by the ordinary, non-confiscatory, property-tax. The rent-seeking (*i.e.*, negative sum gain-seeking) way for individuals to lay claim on local rents is to agitate for government granted entitlements (welfare benefits, excessive political/bureaucratic positions, excessive costs of public sector contracts) financed by taxes in excess of the public-sector cost of public-sector improvements. In practice, the only way such activity can be controlled is by a strict constitutional constraint on a government's ability to use confiscatory taxation/regulation (even here there can be rent-seeking at the constitution-making level which will be less than subsequent rent-seeking costs only if future gains are very uncertain and rent-seekers are very risk-averse and, of course, rent-seeking on judicial interpretation as for example that which effectively eliminated the constraints imposed on US governments by the "takings" clauses in the constitution); something like "The municipality can only tax real property at a rate not to exceed one mil per thousand of market valuation unless approved yearly by a referendum yielding agreement by at least 90% of registered property owners". Such a municipality would only undertake those activities which benefit most of its residents who cared enough about the municipality to at least own some minute portion of property in it (the intent of this might still be diluted by a municipality issuing penny shares in real property within the municipality; some minimum investment should be put at stake to ensure that municipal voters do not act like complete free riders.)

LVT lets the cat in with the canary; it would ultimately destroy the basis for sustainable human settlements and drive market activity to other entitlement margins. This is essentially what happened in the South Bronx as a result of rent controls which are the regulatory equivalent of LVT; dupping [RS: DUP or DUPE activities, as above] would flourish to the limit and consume the equivalent in real resources (private sector rent-seeking which takes place voluntarily by purchases and sales through private asset markets simply transfers an equivalent of asset value using up real resources only to the extent of the brokerage commissions and other relatively minor transactions costs). In short, I definitely do not agree that productive activity, as measured through the market, would necessarily increase if taxes on labour and capital were replaced by taxes on land; I think it would be more likely that market "exchange value" would increase if a tax were placed on all sources of market income (hence, by implication, on all human and non-human wealth generating market income) AT A LOW UNIFORM RATE. M. Friedman suggests that this rate need not exceed ten per cent in order for governments to finance their truly legitimate productive functions (as opposed to redistributional activities which are ultimately illegitimate and immoral since they set faction against faction and lead to the ultimate destruction of the state – and the economy). Historically, prior to the 1940s, this would have been a very high percentage of peacetime governments.

The reason you do not think that LVT is theft must be because you do believe deep down that might makes rights and that the small, elite group of individuals who happen to control any government (even in enlightened democracies and for largely historical reasons) is more worthy of receiving or directing the use of these revenues than the near unanimity of all individuals who have saved the fruits of their productive labour to purchase titles to private property.

Of course, I know you are more of a populist and anti-authoritarian than that – so why would you persist in favouring a device that would enable expropriation of a greater amount in total from the numerous small property investors – home-owners like yourself – than from the relatively few property-developers who often are in hock to financial institutions and pension funds owned by the numerous small stockholders and pensioners?

The Lockean principle is that humans have a right to the proceeds of their [legitimate] labour – all taxes and regula-tions which reduce the value of that labour or of that which can be purchased with such labour (such as goods, services, real or financial assets, bequests to one's progeny and their progeny, etc) infringe on this most basic human right. From this human right, hence, are derived all other bequeathed or earned property-rights!

Odds & Ends:: You are assuming that "scarcity" is perfectly inelastic in supply; however, scarcity is a human creation (as a result of our real preferences for all goods including leisure and our artificial constraints imposed and administered by governments), it has a supply price and a producers and consumer surplus which is legitimately captured by its creators. In aggregate nothing is perfectly elastic or inelastic in supply – meaning there are always infra-marginal and/or quasi rents.

North American Indians had bad immigration laws (as do current Canadians and, without the pass laws, current white South Africans, and Germans and other first worlders subject to invasion by economic refugees, interlopers and other free riders) and they suffered the consequences in the form of hostile take-overs and voluntary exchanges on unfavourable terms (since they only had common-property rights rather than individually-held private property rights no single individual had a net pecuniary individual (as opposed to group) interest in opposing the European takeover). Unfortunately, in the real world effective rights rely on the power (right) to maintain them. The Friedman in the *AER-P&P* was David not Milton. Re smoking: this is one area where my libertarianism and humanitarianism JOINTLY fail. I would not mind at all if capital punishment – or brandishment [sic!] to some far off country or beyond the tail-section – were meted out to every smoker – since they are on the path to self-destruction anyway. For the "social good", why not make it quicker? How is that for a resurgence of the reformist tendencies nascent since learning about public choice in the late 60s??? SKOL ZAS

Date: 11 Oct 1992

From: Zane Spindler
Re: Factional reformism in response to R. Sandilands
You wrote "Reform should be directed to prevention of future deformities." There is a conceptual problem with T&W

[Tollison & Wagner] advocating this since with near perfect foresight or rational expectation, it would merely throw us into another rent-seeking regress which would also not be worthwhile when all the costs are counted.

You wrote "Do you approve of the Indians getting it all back for free? Why not the rest of North America?"

If your car is stolen by a thief (or *de facto* stolen from you by a "mistaken" transfer at the Department of Motor Vehicles) should it be returned to you for free? In most legal cases you have to pay some costs for having your stolen property returned if only those of reporting it stolen and seeking legal redress within a relatively short period of time. The longer the thief (government) possesses the property without you taking action, the stronger her claim – this comes under the law of "adverse possession". Land titles are generally transferred to their possessors after periods ranging from 12-30 years depending on the jurisdiction; cars only take 5-7 years before becoming the property of the current unopposed possessor. In common and statute law, you have to undertake a continuous defence of your property-rights in order to maintain them – in no sense are they free. Academic discussions that ignore this simply demonstrate how little ivory-tower theorists know of *de facto* and *de jure* practice in reality and in law.

The Indians are not getting it back for free since they have paid lobbying and legal costs and currently it costs more for Canadian governments to retain these claims that they are worth in "public possession". In private hands, the land might generate a surplus which the government can always tax as long as it doesn't tax so much as to "kill the goose..." (as a LVT inevitably does – if you can give examples where it appears that it hasn't it is only because appearances are deceptive and it is likely that a good deal of value has been hidden from the tax).

You wrote "But a gradualist introduction of LVT, building up to around, say, 90 per cent after 20 years, would more or less take care of that problem, especially in view of the fact that all landowners would benefit simultaneously from the reduction (ultimately elimination) of all other taxes." Under rational expectations, it matters little whether you introduce a tax gradually or, for its present-value equivalent, immediately, if it is certain it will never be changed in the future. However, as long as legislatures continue in session, laws can always be changed – at a cost, retained – at a cost, or reinstituted – at a cost; all very costly (although probably less so than by direct brute force as with war and pillage for which politics is a substitute (politics is war by other means – to invert Bismarck's famous quote!). The upshot is that gradualist solutions are never completed since they are reversed before complete as part of the normal ebb and flow of the rent-seeking cycle.

You wrote "And remember that LVT isn't really a tax but a user fee which in other contexts you approve." In what possible sense could a LVT be a user fee – it does not compensate for services government provides but rather captures value created largely through private individuals' – as individuals or as a group of individuals – activities; government has a right to capture it only in that it has taken, or been allowed, a partial monopoly over force within a given area of its sovereignty.

You wrote "By the way, LVT would not mean that bureaucrats would own the land. Titles would remain in private hands, but would be conditional upon payment of the user fee." If you live in a house which yields you (say) $1000/month of value, in an area where other similar houses are available to yield similar value to you, and you have two legal options available to you:

a) you pay a "landlord" (perhaps the government) $1000/month to live in that (or any similar and available) house;

b) you are offered a title to a specific house which obligates you to pay the "government" $1000/month for LVT (plus whatever monthly value of renovations you might make as an owner but which are available in the rental market from different houses for which you pay an appropriately higher rent) and to resell the title for the same price (after LVT) as what you originally paid; how much would you pay for option b over option a? In what sense would having such title mean you "owned" the house? Unless you can collect some "surplus" as a "right" from holding a piece of paper called a title, you "own" nothing; to be a "title", a piece of paper (or a common understanding of what constitutes a "right") has to entitle you to something. Pursuit of "Georgian Envy" would be self-impoverishing and societally-impoverishing at the extreme.

Date 31 Oct 92

From: Roger Sandilands
Re: A FOLLOW-UP
... Regarding your main reply:
1. Re privately created amenities and the effect these have on land values. You speak as if all of these are created by landowners *qua* landowners. Land-ownership *per se* is not productive of anything. It can only have implications for distribution, not production. The active factors are labour and capital and the skills and technology they bring to bear to shape and move what nature passively provides in the way of space and resources. Landowners may also be producers, but in their capacity as labourers, capitalist/entrepreneurs, not in their capacity as landowners...

2. 3 percent is a very low social discount rate, but even at that you show not too big a difference between the present discounted value of a 50-year lease compared with 100 years. But my complaint is that even when there is only a small difference between freehold and leasehold, government often prefer to sell freehold because a few thousand extra dollars today is great news to them and damn the future generations "who have done nothing for us"…

3. So yes, the government is often very short-sighted and in the hands of interest groups. So what else is new? So long as we agree there is a need for some minimum government (and I agree with keeping government to a minimum) there is a need to finance its operations. No doubt a government collecting LVT rather than VAT would be just as inept etc. So that's maybe a given. What is not the same is the relative efficiency and equity of LVT *vs* VAT/income taxes, etc.

4. So likewise is the question of the national debt that we saddle future generations with. That's quite separate from the question whether we have LVT or some other form of government revenue. I'm all for "sound money" (within reason).

5. "The market provides an easy test of who should have the rights." LVT DOES use the market test (though I know you are sceptical that professional valuers can correctly identify the market rent. But auctioning of entitlements can also be used). Leases that have to be periodically renewed don't have to involve war. The Hong Kong-China dispute is surely not typical. A lease expires. It's then put up for renewal. The current holder has the right to bid against the market along with everyone else.

6. "With completely surplus exhausting LVT, no one would have an interest in holding such leases." Why ever not? Under LVT a person acquires secure possession and exclusive title

on condition he or she agrees to pay the annual fee or, with a lease, a lump sum that exonerates him from any annual charge during the lifetime of the lease…

Thanks for the O'Rourke piece, though I think it's quite OK for a local community to forego the potential rental income from the property tax on a golf course compared to a forest, if that's where their preferences lie. What is obnoxious is when someone buys the forest at its current use value and then by the stroke of an official's pen it has a completely different value than was expected by all except those willing to engage in bribery and corruption.

With LVT the developer would pay the full rent on the new, maximum PERMITTED use value. His activities as a developer *qua* developer would still be adequately rewarded (under the *impôt unique* there would be no tax on his development work)…

It should be the "community" that decides whether a forest should stay as a forest (or a golf course as a golf course), knowing full well that by prohibiting a more monetarily remunerative use means a sacrifice of revenue. They may rationally prefer that sacrifice, because of non-tangible benefits, etc. But if they do decide they want to change land use then they should change it transparently, in open competition, so that all may share the monetary benefit, not just the corrupt official and his corruptor.

A brief interlude

MY NEXT EXTANT email is not until a year later. However, I have one diary entry, dated 18 October 1993, in which I noted that Zane had been to Bogota to celebrate Lauchlin Currie's

91st birthday on 8 October. Zane had asked me to go with him but I could not get away from teaching. He sent this photo of the party in Currie's office at the Colombian Institute of Savings and Housing.

I HAVE A letter from Currie in which he mentioned Zane's help in drawing up a summary of the implications of a paper on

"endogenous growth" that Currie was finishing at that time. Currie died in December 1993 and this paper was later published in the *History of Political Economy*, 1997).

Date: 18 Nov 1993

From: Zane Spindler
Re: [no subject line]

"Value is what it is thought to be" just like "money is accepted because it is accepted". I think you are more in danger of sounding like an "English Gentleman" (*i.e.*, an aristocratic snob) who looks down his nose at those "in the trade"** (*i.e.*, the *nouveau riche* who threaten his exalted position), than like a Marxist (although both suffer from an excess of romanticism). If it were not for "brokering" services, broadly defined, Singapore would still be just another Kampong. (As professors, aren't we brokering knowledge?)

I would have thought you would favour the sort of redistribution undertaken by Singapore through its housing policy. The "Taking" involved is more concentrated among an unpopular, possibly more unproductive, few; is much less extensive than "Taking" in other countries; and the policy on balance has probably enhanced Singapore's overall productivity. However, as usual, your point is well taken, that Singapore is not perfectly free (and certainly Milton is going to find this result that Singapore AND Hong Kong are EQUALLY FREE, and Freeest, hard to stomach since he admonished Singapore about its policies on at least one occasion. As one who is currently dabbling in economic Darwinism, I guess I'd have to find favour with their policy(ies) because they have succeeded – so far!

RegardZS

** There is a great scene on this in "Remains of the Day". Have you seen this movie yet? It is really well done. Also, "The Joy Luck Club" is extremely worth viewing – if you bring a box of Kleenex.

Diary 12 December 1994

Zane and I have resumed our debate over land value taxation, and he is losing patience with my "dogged" attachment to nineteenth century classical thinking. I accuse him of blind attachment to the obfuscations of twentieth century neo-classical economics.

In today's message he says that "land does not exist until it has value", and urged me to substitute the word "diamonds" for land, to see where that would lead me. I retorted that diamonds in the ground are part of Nature – land. Diamonds in the shop are commodities that are produced by men through their labour, combined with man-made capital, that have value because of the marginal costs of production in conjunction with the demand schedule. But that intra-marginal mines can yield up their treasures for less cost, and so yield a surplus called rent. And so on.

But I was contemplating breaking off our exchanges altogether in the face of his response to my telling him of Vilfredo

Pareto's fascist, illiberal philosophy that dismisses any concern for the poor as being poor eugenics. Zane agrees with Pareto! Well, I sent him Mason Gaffney's article on the distinguishing characteristics of land, and hope that Zane will read it and comment. He is bound to dismiss it as a diatribe, but I shall be interested in the other reasons he gives. It seems that neither of us will convince the other, but will only help the other to sharpen his own defences.

Date: 8 Dec 1994

From: Zane Spindler
Re: [no subject provided]
[RS: This alludes to a previous email in which I mention Mason Gaffney's two new books, viz. *The Corruption of Economics* and *Land and Taxation*. I wrote that Gaffney catalogues the political background to the university appointment of people like J B Clark and Seligman and R T Ely (founder of the AEA) and how they developed the marginalist revolution as a counter to the classical economists' focus on land as a separate factor of production, distinct from man-mad capital, etc etc, and so diverting attention from "incentive taxation" of the Ricardian surplus.]

He really lays into Ely and Knight and Pareto (an out-and-out fascist; ironic how we associate his name with "optimality"), etc. I was rather disconcerted to read about Ely's life and work, because he was Allyn Young's teacher, and co-author of the famous *Outlines of Economics*. But I always wondered about him since comparing the 1923 edition, which Young had much to do with the 1930 edition which Young only read up to about chapter 12, and not the chapter on land and rent, which differs greatly from the 1923 edition and swallows the Clarkian line totally whereas the earlier editions were much less hostile to the single tax. In his LSE lectures Young says "there is much to be said for the single tax", but cautiously. Lauchlin was close to Young on the land question: preferring the Mill approach to the George approach, but putting much emphasis anyway on the "unearned increment" view of things.

Zane replies:

I would be interested in Gaffney's stuff.

However, a basic understanding of value… that it arises from and is created by, and does not exist apart from, human desires … would quickly eliminate any inclination to speak of "unearned increments" or "unearned surplus". Further, an elementary understanding of rent-seeking would eliminate any inclination to speak of "Surplus". [People speak of such things out of an inclination to manipulate the political agenda, not from purely theoretical motives.]

From the R-S perspective, the "single tax" is just another rent-seeking vehicle which may exhaust some momentary "surplus" in the rent-seeking competition such an imaginary surplus elicits. Since in practice the ST will not necessarily skew the distribution your way or toward the general interest or necessarily improve efficiency given its non-lump sum nature in practice (we are then into second best puzzles), I am still amazed by your dogged devotion to that issue. However, I still hope to collect some payoff myself from your enthusiasm, by writing a paper derived from our correspondence (even though experience shows such activity on my part, *ex post*, over-exhausts prospective rents).

RJS quote: "… Pareto (an out-and-out fascist; ironic how we associate his name with "optimality")" No irony at all if you understand that fascism is just the epitome of interventionism

(Keynesianism, Georgism, Currieism, etc). As the saying goes: "Scratch a (current-day) Liberal (Socialist, Communist, etc) and you will find a Fascist lurking underneath the skin." Like other good current-day liberals, Hitler was just another do-gooder out to establish a perfect (optimal) world. He was also a vegetarian!

Date: 9 December 1994 12:22:05.21

From: Roger Sandilands
Re: [no subject provided]
Dear Zane:

Should I rise to the bait and reopen our old debate, "doggedly"? Out of altruistic (look the word up in the dictionary; I think it still exists) interest in your rent-seeking publications efforts on rent-seeking/ dissipation, I shall re-enter the fray (actually, of course, it was I who deliberately got you going again with my last message/ diatribe). Yes, of course it is only "we" (people) who create land values, as is true of any values, by desiring or demanding effectively. But we did not create or produce the land itself – the "free gift of nature". Since land itself (as distinct from the improvements upon it) was not produced, any price or value attaching to land is a reflection of pure scarcity only. Land's existence does not depend on its value. The price paid (either the freehold price or the annual rent) is a pure transfer payment, unlike, say, the price paid for [...Message was aborted here, and continued in next message.]

9 December 1994 13:04:53.15

From: Roger Sandliands

Re: surplus rejoined

Land transactions as Transfer payments?

Land is purchased or rented because it is expected to yield value when it is used. But when we do produce things with our labour and capital in association with the land, those things themselves have value. Some of that value compensates labour and capital. Some is captured by land. How much goes to land depends on how "intra-marginal" the site is. How intra-marginal it is will depend not on the physical properties or its location, and not on its (real) costs of production, which is zero, but on the strength of competition for it. Land does have an opportunity cost, but not a real cost.

In what sense can it be said that a rise in rents reflects land's contribution to growth of GDP? There is no more land than last year, or a million years ago. Output can grow only if the fixed stock of land is acted upon by labour and capital using known technologies and processes. So, together, the latter variables determine the growth of output, but land captures some of the increment, which means that the factors that do contribute to growth get less than they produce, just because land is not limitless or homogeneous. Land has to be priced in order that it be rationed amongst competing uses, but the question of efficient pricing has to be kept separate from the question of efficient and/or "just" distribution.

The taxation of land values does, as you emphasise, necessitate knowing the market-clearing price, and there is scope for bribing the valuation officers or for fixing the auction process. But these are surely not insurmountable or fatal objections. Similar objections apply to the taxation of wages or interest income, or sales taxes. But, on the principle of "if it moves don't tax it", and the converse, LVT has it. (A nice Dickensian flourish!)

Re Pareto, Gaffney catalogues his fascist credentials not to paint him as an interventionist but for the opposite: he was an ardent neo-classical exponent in the sense that he objected to any kind of intervention designed to improve the lot of the poorer members of society, on the grounds that the poor are poor because inferior, and to help them is bad eugenics.

9 December 1994

From: Zane Spindler
RE: surplus rejoined
Roger,
If…
"Pareto was characterised as a fascist not because of his interventionist tendencies but for the opposite: he was an ardent neo-classical exponent in the sense that he objected to any kind of intervention designed to improve the lot of the poorer members of society, on the grounds that the poor are poor because inferior, and to help them is bad eugenics."

Then, he was not a fascist but a classical liberal who, unlike today's liberals, could face the facts as scientific observation revealed them, rather than the fantasies one wishes were so. Using a modern buzzword, he might now say that helping the poor can be "unsustainable" eugenics… as well as unsustainable politics.

Date: 9 December 1994

From: Zane Spindler
RE: Land

Dear Roger,

Glad you have rejoined the debate albeit at the same point we started at several years ago.

RJS: "But we did not create or produce the land itself – the "free gift of nature". Since land itself (as distinct from the improvements upon it) was not produced, any price or value attaching to land is a reflection of pure scarcity only. Land's existence does not depend on its value."

You know, Roger, this sort of nonsense could only be propagated by academics, or others who have never spent any time creating value, in general, or value associated with land, in particular. There is no "free gift of nature"; land (or, in general, so-called "natural resources" which are un-natural in the sense they would be never known or valued without human enterprise) must be "developed" before it yields value. "Scarcity" is not natural but is created by humans' desires and their competitive enterprise motivated by their desires. To use land requires its "defense" from others who also wish to use it; this is a (opportunity) cost (hence, value… remember your double-entry accounting) imputed and borne by humans. This value does not come as a "free gift of nature" but as a result of active human imagination (the most important and, hence, most highly valued component) and human action.

Land's existence does indeed depend on its value. This is most obvious for the case of (un) natural resources, but it applies to every other valued "land" as well. Just for the fun of it, try calling "diamonds" "land" (which they are) and everyplace you have written "land" write "diamonds" instead; then read it through to see just how much sense your LVT stuff makes.

I think you will have to transcend the 19th century thinking of the Classical economists and their ilk, before you can understand the irrelevance of a "full valued" LVT.

Date: 12 December 1994

From: Roger Sandilands
Re: Land

Zane:

"Land's existence does indeed depend on its value." Wow! Have you been addled by the neo-classical fusion of the factor land with the man-made factor of capital. You have it completely the wrong way round. Land value depends on the existence of land. And it is indeed created by man's efforts and desires. But land is not created by man, and land exists and has existed since time immemorial whatever its value or price as put upon it by man.

You still cannot accept that whereas man creates land value that value was only tangentially created by the owners of the sites with the value, rather than by the competitive pressure of aggregate effective demand beating against a fixed total of land and natural resources. Diamonds in the ground are part of nature, and so are included in the classical definition of land. And they are free gifts insofar as they exist independently of man.

Diamonds dripping from the ears of my wife are, however, man-made commodities and have value equal to the marginal costs of extracting them from diamond mines and fashioning, shaping and transporting them to the final consumer. Their supply as commodities is not fixed. But some are more easily obtained than others, and the owners of the diamond mines that are more easily mined enjoy a rent equal to the difference between their costs of labour and capital and the marginal costs of the marginal mine in operation (which in turn is a function of the strength of demand for diamonds).

Diamonds in the ground have always existed. Their existence has nothing to do with the value placed on diamonds in the shops.

Land too exists independently of its value. Its value depends on the demand for it relative to the fixed supply. Its value does not depend on the efforts of the owners as such, as individuals. If I did not exist, the land on which my house sits would still be as valuable as it is. It is essential that land has a value that reflects its relative scarcity, for in that way it is put to its best use. That is the allocative function of price. But it is not necessary that we accept the distributive consequences of landowners capturing these values rather than the community that created them.

What I object to is having to hand over part of my hard-earned wages as taxes. My wages belong to me by right of work. Taxation is theft. Rent does not belong to landowners by right but by virtue of historical "right of first possession", frontier style, and subsequent man-made laws to protect private property for the initial seizers and their direct or indirect heirs. To introduce a levy for the right of continued occupancy and use of any particular site on, under, or above ground would restore these values from god-given land and natural resources. It is a levy, fee, or price, rather than a tax, because the benefit principle applies directly. It is ethically and eugenically obviously RIGHT. Once you have shuffled off the veil of twentieth century neo-classical obfuscation you will return to the old verities. Yea, the trumpet will ring, and ring, and ring. And on judgment day will ye be judged, verily sayeth I. I Ching. CheeRS

Date: 13 December 1994

From: Roger Sandilands
Re: Land
Well, Zane, you should be well on your way to an article for the *AER* on the survival theory of economic truth and rent

dissipation.I have to spend time this morning on the theory of overlapping generations for a PhD viva this afternoon, so will only make a couple of comments today.

On the obfuscation insult, I was simply retaliating in less diplomatic words, for your statement that I must "transcend the nineteenth century thinking of the classical economists and their ilk. On the value of my house: yes its value will be greater for the improvements we have made to it. That's known as a return to labour and capital. What I have not done is anything that has increased (or decreased) the value of the site on which it sits. Nor did I create the site value that existed when I bought the house on that site. Nor did the original discoverers of that bit of land, nor the succession of owners and occupiers since that time. If it had been fenced off since the beginning and never used, its value today would be just about the same as it is.

I hope you enjoy Mason Gaffney's paper when it arrives. I look forward to your comments on it. It should allow you to finish your piece for the *AER*. The dominant neo-classical "fusionists" ("land is no different from capital") who guide the profession will be delighted with it.

Finally, I thought you might enjoy the following:

By a fundamental law of our minds… we cannot conceive of a means without an end; a contrivance without an object…. Unless man himself may rise to or bring forth something higher, his existence is unintelligible. So strong is this metaphysical necessity that those who deny to the individual anything more than this life are compelled to transfer the idea of perfectibility to the race.

But there is nothing whatever to show any essential race improvement. Human progress is not the improvement of human nature. The advances in which civilization consists are not secured in the constitution of man, but in the constitution of society. They are thus not fixed and permanent, but may at any time be lost—nay, are constantly tending to be lost. [*Progress and Poverty*, Ch.27]

CheeRS.

PS: Singapore's reclaimed land is capital fashioned out of land. It demands a return on the capital alone.

Date: 13 December 1994

From: Zane Spindler
Re: Land

You write:

"What I have not done is anything that has increased (or decreased) the value of the site on which it sits. Nor did I create the site value that existed when I bought the house on that site. Nor did the original discoverers of that bit of land, nor the succession of owners and occupiers since that time. If it had been fenced off since the beginning and never used, its value today would be just about the same as it is."

Come on, Roger. You are a bit over the top here. Suppose 2000 years ago your neighbourhood – or all of Glasgow – had been fenced off as a totally untouchable forestry reserve for all eternity. Your lot's value would be literally priceless or valueless, but certainly not the same as without this man-made restriction. This is quite clear from the history of the ALR (NDP imposed Agricultural Land Reserve) in the Fraser Valley. Again, I don't think your statement above is quite right and I think you might see it more clearly if you lived in a less homogeneous country like the US. (Although the UK has become less homogeneous.)

I think you, and the potential buyers and previous owners like you, did create the unique site value of your house and each has shared in that value in proportion to their contribution. Presumably, you were successful in obtaining your house because you offered better terms than other potential buyers and more favourable terms than the reserve price of the previous owner; the selling price thus was equal to the reserve price plus the premium you were willing to pay over that reserve price to obtain possession of that house yourself... that was your contribution to the house/ site value. Now if your neighbourhood is like mine, you may also have noticed that your neighbours spend a lot of time discussing neighbourhood improvements and morally and legally disciplining wayward neighbours. Neighbourhoods where such self-serving "public-spiritedness" does not occur, soon fall into decay with an accompanying cascade of site values (until regentrified or redeveloped at a profit to the labour and capital of the farsighted). Hayek, or someone, once said of rent controls that they were the surest of destroying a city next to bombing [*Editors' note*: actually the quote is from Assar Lindbeck, 1971].

I think the same could probably be said of LVT because it would tax those largely unseen, individual contributions of labour and capital that create valuable and livable communities. This is painfully obvious in many places such as the South Bronx, Leningrad and other places where individuals' pride of ownership was taken away or sorely taxed.

CheerZS

PS: On the "...dominant neo-classical "fusionists" ("land is no different from capital") who guide the profession...".

I am unaware of such a professional ideoarchy; if there is, I may be in trouble (by not saying anything new). But to get a better view of why the so called gifts of nature are not free, read John Umbeck's classic study of California gold miners in his *Western Economic Journal* (1971, I believe) article "Might makes Rights" [RS: Actually it was in *Economic Inquiry*, 1981] or read about the Oklahoma "free land" rush and its accompanying costs.[On the above quote from Henry George's *Progress and Poverty*]

Well, I agree that each generation much is lost; but more optimistically, I think much more is gained and that, on balance, humanity has improved, primarily because individual humans have improved as the underlying basis for any improvement in human societies.

Ask yourself whether you would have been better off during any other period in history ... past or future. probably "no" for the former, hopefully "yes" for the latter.

Date: 4 January 1995

From: Zane Spindler
Re: Whose Quote?

I read your MG [Mason Gaffney] article on the way down here and enjoyed it… It gave me extra insight into the error in Georgists' ways. (I say this not only because MG carries on like an evangelist acting as if any other belief system must be pathological, but also because there seems to be some fundamental inconsistencies in his position; *e.g.*, contrast Sec. A7 with B8).

I was quite interested to note that he has moved from the traditional concept of land (as a geographical hard surface location, *i.e.*, not water or air) to a potential modern concept of land as space (not only physical, but also notional as in intellectual property-rights; while physical space is fixed – at infinity – notional space is infinitely variable).

Unfortunately, too often when he refers to land in this way – which is really just a concept of anything over which humans have (or will) define property-rights, he sounds as if he still has the physical variety in mind.

Further, he is not geographically up-to-date, as he doesn't recognise that geographical and astronomical forces may be most often slow relative to Man's time on earth – but not always, as the seasons, earthquakes, hurricanes, tornados, floods and natural fires too often remind us. More important, when people move, or their ideas (tastes) change, together, land/ space value changes apace.

These agglomeration effects are fascinating to 20th century economists, but, as macroeconomists have discovered to their chagrin, they are as uncontrollable as the "Acts of God" cited above; indeed, that is more their nature as no one has explained why markets boom or crash (and why they don't) except by reference to human passions or the sociology of conventionalism. Even "catastrophe theory" has not answered the crucial ontological questions; ie, why do these surfaces fold where they do anyway? "Chaos Theory" also fails here. Both are descriptive not predictive.

We do know, however, that "The Law of Unintended Consequences" holds and would surely make fools of any Georgians in command as it did for Keynesians. The simple fact is that if the LVT assessor cannot predict the rents before the rest of the market, there will be no rents left to capture – only capitalised costs which LVT would shift around in indeterminate ways.

Anyway, I've made lots of marginal comments on my copy, thereby, invalidating it as a reference for my students. Reading Gaffney's version of George, I was struck by the geographical and cultural relativism embedded in George's positions: Would

George have been a Georgist if he had lived in Outer Mongolia rather than the turn-of-the-last-century US [RS: George died in 1897] or if he had grown up in my cousin's family? (Her mother always used to rave about how they were "land poor".)Her grandfather had foreclosed on his neighbouring farmers during the depression and her father subsequently struggled his entire life as a farmer and trapper to earn enough from all that land to be able to pay their taxes.

Now that her parents have died she is going to let all the land go back to prairie-seed under a state programme that excuses taxes for such land allocations. A more imaginative, less nostalgia-driven entrepreneur would look at that property [adjacent to a major lake and 20-30 highway miles from medium size, high income cities] as a gold mine if properly developed as high-end recreational property – but not if the value would be stolen by the taxman.

Bottom Line: Entrepreneurs (not raw land) create locational value. However, you will be pleased to know there is a practising Georgian in South Africa in the person of Jannie de Graft [sic; Jan van de Graf] (the brilliant author of that slim 1957 volume on Welfare Economics). Brian Kantor relates from a conversation with de Graft that the family fortune (large enough so he doesn't have to practice economics) has been derived from selling land as the city advances and buying further out to resell in the future. So there you have it – Henry George's LVT assessor – privatized. Why should he get the loot rather than the public (*i.e.*, public-sector rent-seekers like you and me)? Because he is smarter.

Incidentally, have you read *The Bell Curve* yet? Don't let the politically correct reviewers put you off. It is a book every true scholar should read.

CheerZS

Date: 3 Apr 1997

From: Zane Spindler
Re: G B Shaw understood public choice...?
Roger
I finished Phang's article [Phang Sock Yong, "Economic Development and the Distribution of Land Rents in Singapore: A Georgist Implementation", *American J. of Economics and Sociology*, Oct.1996] which was interesting in that it supported the point I will make in my "Henry George after Gordon Tullock" article, if I ever finally sit down to write it (I am getting close!), that the rents are dissipated by competition for them whether they are left with the landlord or extracted by government (and dispersed in line with pressure group competition) unless the rule of law or meritocratic government directs such competition toward less resource-using forms (*i.e.* voluntary auctions for ALL allocations substitute asset transfers for resource-using rent-seeking).

Your point that taxing land rents is better than taxing incomes seems to be supported, given low income tax rates conventionally defined (but not if CPF [Central Provident Fund] "taxes" are included) and high growth rates, except that the crucial factors are really the savings/investment rates and that the Government of Singapore takes up such a small fraction of GDP. If it was like Sweden's govt, income tax rates would be much higher and growth much lower.

If land development generates externalities in the form of higher property values experienced by other (perhaps non-developing) landholders, these externalities are really mutually captured by landholders over time as incentives exist for uniform development which in turn are reflected in differential rates of appreciation of land values.

It seems that a Georgist would not be satisfied with such appreciation being captured by landowners as a class distinct from the general population. But suppose that the general population is composed of only landowners (as is coming to be the case in Singapore)? Would a Georgist's redistributionist bent have to be much different or at least without the political appeal of taking from Peter to pay Paul given that Paul is really Peter?

Further, such redistribution would encourage free-riding and rent-seeking on the part of non-residents who would have an incentive to immigrate to an LVT local to dissipate the rents distributed through the public sector. Here Singapore, once again, sets another sterling example of minimizing rent-seeking by limiting immigration, both from current generations abroad and future generations within. Without such limits, the tragedy of the commons would befall any regime which relied on LVT relatively more than other regimes or all regimes using LVT with respect to migration from the future (ie. excessive birth rates, eg. India after landlords were expropriated). CheerZS

Date: 7 June 99

ZANE SENT ME the following "Tale" (see previous email) and here asks me (and his SFU students) questions on it.

A Tale of Twin Cities: A Parable in Urban Political Economy!

ONCE UPON A time, there was a factory at Edge where twelve people worked together as a team. When all twelve team members were present, one thousand ducats of output was produced every hour, but when even one team member was missing, nothing was produced.

Six of the workers, Edgeans, lived in the city, Edge, next to the factory. The other six workers, Knollites, lived in the "suburbs" at Knoll, across a deep chasm, with a raging river, that was spanned by a primitive, rope-suspension bridge. If one Knollite worker attempted to cross the bridge, it took only ten minutes; if all six attempted to cross at once, it took a total of twenty minutes for all six to reach the other side, and the bridge appeared to be quite congested in the meanwhile. Knollite workers always chose to cross the bridge together with each experiencing, in common, a twenty-minute commute between their homes and their work, morning and evening.

A traveling, troubadour economist noticed this congestion and calculated that, by crossing the bridge at the same time, all Knollite workers were imposing a total congestion cost on themselves of fourteen ducats per day (seven ducats each morning and evening). He proposed a toll of ten ducats for anyone who attempted to cross the bridge while anyone else was on it. Given the differing marginal value of time for each of the Knollite workers, this new toll, which no Knollite worker chose to pay, cut congestion to nil. Unfortunately, it also now took an hour, rather than twenty minutes, for the six Knollite workers to all cross the bridge.

Initially, that delayed assembly of the entire team, and production, by forty minutes, foregoing eight hundred ducats of production. It also caused the six Edgeans workers to waste forty minutes of time waiting for all six Knollite workers to finally assemble at the factory. Using their respective wages rates, Edgean workers valued that time loss at a total of forty-two ducats.

Thus, the first day of the congestion toll, there was a total loss, and marginal social cost of imposing it, of eight hundred and forty-two ducats, even though the measured loss, as recorded in the Gross Knoll-Edge Product (GKP) accounts, was only eight hundred ducats. Naturally, everyone, including the team leader (an Edgean), noticed that they were worse off that day.

The team leader got very upset. She told the Knollite workers that they all had to show up on time at the start of the next production day. Consequently, following a schedule suggested by the troubadour-economist (after reference to the respective wage rates for Knollite workers), the four lowest-paid Knollite workers voluntarily avoided the toll by rising, and crossing the bridge, at various times earlier in the day, and later at night. Given this rational, self-interested, and, incidentally, community-spirited action of those four, one of the remaining two Knollite workers (the second-highest paid), maintained his routine of leaving and arriving home at the same time, while the other, final Knollite worker (the highest paid), got to leave home ten minutes later and arrive home ten minutes earlier.

Consequently, the next and subsequent days, the highest-paid Knollite benefitted from the toll, the second-highest-paid Knollite experienced no net change in wellbeing, and four lowest-paid Knollites suffered a loss in wellbeing. The net amount all Knollites suffered was now calculated by the troubadour-economist, using the Knollite workers' respective wage rates (which the economist assumed to be equal to their marginal values of time), at approximately nine ducats per day in total, which, he noted, was much less than the fourteen ducats of congestion costs saved per day.

This calculation ignored information unavailable to the troubadour-economist at the time. First, the four Knollite team members became sleep-deprived which eventually caused the value of team production and GKP to fall by a few ducats per day. Second, some Knollite workers reevaluated their decision to live in Knoll, rather than by the factory in Edge. They moved to Edge, thereby displacing some non-working Edge dwellers to Knoll, and causing house prices and land values to rise in Edge and to fall in Knoll. As a result, there were (approximately balanced) capital gains and losses, and also crossmigration moving costs of one hundred ducats, albeit only the latter were true social costs. Finally, there was the prospect that in order to insure survival of the honor system with respect to crossing the bridge one at a time, and to collect any tolls arising from noncompliance, one of the Edgean workers might have had to be hired for an hour, at two ducats per hour, to monitor the crossing, morning and evening, for a total cost of four ducats per day.

All these unintended consequences were not foreseen by the troubadour-economist who, only looking at observable, now negligible, bridge congestion and observable, as yet unchanged, GKP, thought he had done a marvellous job.

One Knollite tried to argue with the troubadour-economist, remarking that a toll monitor might have to be hired. But the troubadour-economist said even in that eventuality, there would still be a net social gain from his congestion-toll innovation -- albeit, it would be much smaller at one ducat per day rather than five ducats per day.

The Knollite persisted that if that monitor used her market power as the lowest paid Edgean to go on strike for higher wages, she could force her hourly wage up toward that of the next highest-paid Edgean, thereby doubling monitoring costs to as much as eight ducats per day and turning the perceived welfare gain into a welfare loss. Also, since no toll revenues were raised by the economist's congestion-eliminating, prospective toll, another toll would have to be levied for every bridge crossing just to cover those monitoring costs, and that toll itself would cause congestion.

The economist laughed and said that in such a small community, social pressure would preclude the need for monitoring and, if not, the unfettered greed of the Edgean monitor would be controlled by competition from the lowest paid Knollite. Since this Knollite worker was awake and crossing the bridge earlier than her fellow bridge users, she could also monitor the bridge. But, the argumentative Knollite persisted, would a Knollite monitor do that, rather than colluding with other Knollites to ignore or strike against all tolls, or to collude with the Edgean monitor to raise the monitoring wage?

If that happens, the troubadour-economist said, a lump-sum tax (LST) could simply be levied on all residents of Knoll, or on Knoll property, to pay for the Edgean monitor without resorting to a congestion-causing collection of tolls. Such a tax could always be raised to cover any wage demands of Edgean monitors. It could even be raised to cover the total cost of any size bureaucracy necessary to monitor the monitors.

The economist thought that the main effect of such an LST would be to redistribute wealth and income from Knollites to Eadgeans, perhaps thereby giving an incentive for Knollites to become Edgeans for a further saving of Knollite commuting costs. The effects of the LST on the efficiency of bridge use or production would be minimal, if not beneficial, he claimed. In fact, he said, total GKP would rise by the inclusion of the wage costs of the monitoring bureaucrats, if such monitoring was made necessary by the toll-induced failure of (the previously costless) community norms. Given the impossibility of privately dissuading the troubadour-economist from his tolling scheme with reasoned argument, the suffering Knollites resorted to politics.

Being a democratic community that decided its common actions by unanimous referenda, the four "locationally- and distributionally-disadvantaged" Knollites signed a petition to put to a referendum the following proposition: "Proposition T-E: Resolved that the troubadour-economist NOT be Stoned to Death." (Stoning was a customary punishment for social deviants in this community). Although all Edgeans and Knollites were eligible to vote, only five Knollites showed up at the poll, and only one of them voted in favour of the proposition. The proposition thereby failed to achieve unanimity, and the troubadour-economist was summarily stoned to death and dropped in the chasm by the petition-signers.

Then all Knollites, using a dominant assurance contract, formed a club which built a congestion-free bridge. They had previously been indifferent between internalizing minor, shared, congestion costs and the shared costs of investing in a better bridge. But they now realized that any damned fool stranger might again come around and suggest solutions to the observable congestion without calculating all the unobservable and unanticipated, transitional and eventual, private and social costs of their solutions. The option value of avoiding future foolishness tipped the balance in favor of the privately-owned, and keyed, bridge.

One expected consequence of the new bridge was that all Knollite workers had an extra twenty minutes per day (ten minutes morning and evening) to spend on their hobbies, improve their homes, and/ or to get more sleep. The associated, unexpected consequence of this extra time was that, being happier, better housed, and less sleep deprived, the Knollites became more effective team members, thereby raising both production, GKP, and their wages.

Further, club members were pleased to discover they were able to defray some of their costs by renting their keys, when they were not using them, to non-club members who found it worthwhile to pay a premium to use the private, rather than the public, bridge. These key-rental payments for a productive service might have expanded the measured GKP, if declared as income, and since there was no income tax and, hence, no tax penalty for doing so, this came to be the case.

These events, and the congestion toll, passed into history without anyone noticing that the lowest paid Knollite threw approximately four times the number of stones as the other stoning, and distributionally-disadvantaged, Knollites. Nor was any troubadour-economist on hand, then or later, to figure out the necessary and sufficient conditions that guaranteed such an outcome!

That one unfortunate and gruesome event, and the subsequent voluntary private problem-solving, provided a "signal" to troubadour-economists that it was in their interest to avoid Knoll-Edge. Thus, congestion tolls, lump-sum taxes, and troubadour-economists, were precluded from Knoll-Edge forever.

QUESTIONS: (for aspiring public finance, urban and/or transportation economists):

1. Was the congestion toll a Pareto improvement?

2. What was the cumulative net social value of the troubadour-economist during his stay in Knoll-Edge?

3. Were Knoll-Edgeans rational voters, and, if so, were they instrumental or expressive voters?

4. Could the tragic death of the troubadour-economist have been avoided by the "winners" from his schemes compensating the "losers"?

5. Bonus Question! What were the initial Knollite wage rates (to the nearest two ducats)?

Date: Sept 30, 2000

From: Zane Spindler

Re: The Madness of our Rulers [re P.E. Trudeau]

Not only the weather has made this a somber weekend.

We have witnessed the passing of perhaps the greatest Canadian of this last, or any other, century.

For the current generation of students, and like with JFK for the US, it is difficult to portray the excitement created by this man for those Canadians who were caught up by his magic at the time.

His charisma was in tune with the fervor of his times, and thereby he energized and empowered the Federal government to undertake programs that fundamentally changed the economic and political nature of Canada, for better or worse, for richer or poorer, as the saying goes in another context.

Perhaps Trudeau, himself, stated it best when he said:

"We are going to be governed whether we like it or not...We must therefore concern ourselves with politics...to mitigate as far as possible the damage done by the madness of our rulers." Pierre Elliot Trudeau (Canadian Prime Minister, 1968-84).

While it is said that "it is bad to speak ill of the dead", the inevitable assessments of Trudeau's contributions to Canada will be made and some, like the *National Post* Commentary attached to this email, will not be very favorable.

There are, however, lessons to be drawn and learned from these analyses, especially for students in policy and other economics courses. While the culture, the institutions and the structure of an economy and a government are perhaps the dominant determinants of a nation's success over time, occasionally an individual politician can make a substantial difference, especially when they have the personal power to change structures, institutions and cultures.

For many years after Trudeau-mania subsided, one of my favorite comparisons was Trudeau versus Lee Kuan Yew, the Singaporean leader who I had an opportunity to observe when I spent a year as a visiting professor at the National University around the time of Trudeau's last government. Both were charismatic leaders who had vaguely similar backgounds (both lawyers trained at, among other places, Cambridge and LSE -- then the elite schools for intellectual radicals) and both were the dominant political characters in their countries during their times.

However, they did not share similar economic visions. As a result, one country enjoyed an unprecedented rise from poverty to prosperity, while the other fell from prosperity to mediocrity, during their respective tenures.

Of course, these were not singlehanded accomplishments. Each leader relied on advisors who (especially the plethora of competing advisors in Canada) enthusiastically lobbied for their favorite schemes midst ongoing political turmoil over appropriate public policy.

But one leader chose wisely, the other did not.

So, extending Trudeau's pragmatic political action paradigm in the quote above, "we must therefore concern ourselves with"... the "madness" of leaders' advisors and policy wonks -- and the "madness" of our times.

Date: March 6, 2002

From: Zane Spindler
Re: Japanese Universities
Roger,
Incidentally, if you do come to Japan, do not plan to bring or receive cheques here -- in yen or other currencies.

Here is a story of my experience:

I received a Thomas Cook cheque issued by Global Payments "Payable of Presentation to: Sumitomo Mitsui Banking Corporation" for a total of 12,614 Japanese Yen in payment for the review that I did for a UK publisher.

This was some time back, but I just got around to trying to cash it at my own bank (CitiBank). They said that I had to deposit the cheque and have it cleared before I could draw cash on it. So I filled out the deposit forms, waited for my number to come up, went to the counter and gave them to the teller. She said CitiBank would charge me 620 Yen to clear the cheque and that she would have to call Sumitomo to find out what they would charge, please sit down and wait til I call you. Which I did for about half an hour until I thought "This is ridiculous, I could wait all day -- and indeed, I could have, because when I went up to the counter I found that they were just waiting for the other bank to return their call. So I said: "Where is the other bank?" They said it was just a few floors lower in the building. So I said: "Okay, I will go there directly and present the cheque as directed to the above named bank".

Unfortunately, they also would not cash it directly. Instead, they insisted it must first be deposited into an account, and then after some period of time, the account would be credited with the amount of the cheque minus their fee of 2500 Yen (On a 12,000 Yen cheque). I pointed out that these conditions were not written on the cheque and that cheques were normally cleared at par in most developed banking systems. In reply, I was told that this is the way it is done in Japan. I replied that Japanese banks must then be run by Yakuza (The Japanese Mafia) because this amounted to a holdup. The whole exchange was funny in its own cross cultural way.But "That's the way we do things in Japan."

As a banking employee explained numerous times to every argument I made. His bank had no appreciation for the principle of "clearing at par" nor felt under any legal obligation to do so. So I sent the cheque back to be reissued in Canadian dollars. You will find amazing cartel type arrangements here that guarantee that everyone gets a little piece of every action.

CheerZS

Date: March 16, 2002

From: Roger Sandilands
Re: Land Rents

Check out D. Gale Johnson's article in the latest issue of *REE*. Yes; most interesting, though also misleading in some respects:

1. He does not demonstrate to my satisfaction that population growth caused the increase in agricultural productivity, as opposed to being its result. I think he downplays the way that population growth, by depressing wages, delays the adoption of labour-saving methods. Nevertheless, I strongly agree that increased demand for food (a function of rising incomes more than an increased number of mouths to feed; he tends to equate increased need with increased real effective demand) stimulates an increase in productivity -- the Allyn Young theory of self-sustaining growth. Allyn Young, by the way, in the 1920s powerfully rejected the anxieties of the elasticity of supply pessimists -- see Mehrling & Sandilands (eds.), Ch. 20 "Our wealth in cereals". He too insisted that the 'law' of diminishing returns has a built-in tendency to be endogenously offset. By the way, a few years ago I had some very cordial correspondence with Theodore Schultz on Allyn Young and Currie, and he referred to it - and my biography of LC - in his last book on Increasing Returns.

2. Population growth may boost GDP, but several empirical studies suggest it is negatively associated with GDP per capita. It's the latter that matters to all except the Catholics and Muslims who think that the more people there are to populate heaven the better, regardless of the effect on poverty in this life.

3. He repeats the Julian Simon idea that the more people the more knowledge, therefore the more the better. I think this is plain dumb.

4. Yes; the share of agricultural land rents in national income has declined in the US, thanks to land-saving innovations. But the *underlying* rentals are higher, in the sense that because of the increased share of GDP taken from labour and capital in taxes, the amount that can be paid for land is lower than it would be if taxes were abolished and instead the government relied on the collection of land rents as the 'natural' source of state finance (and its natural constraint on the size of government). In other words, it is necessary to look below the surface for the ultimate incidence of taxes, as the physiocrats well understood.

5. While agricultural rents are a very small share of GDP, it is important to recognise that non-agricultural land is still very important. What is the rental value of Manhattan? What would the rental value of Manhattan be if all taxes were abolished and replaced by land rents for state revenue?

CheeRS

Date: 21 Oct 04

From: Zane Spindler
Re: Even a chef cannot unscramble eggs, but must continue making his 'omelette'
Hi Roger,

Thanks for the Jenkins article which gives an interesting, if twisted, reason to support Bush over Kerry, though it may be based as much on fantasy as that claimed for neocons. Reality often turns out to be more like what people want it to be when they care enough to make it happen. Who cared more about their own vision of Europe/Asia, Hitler/Hirohito or Roosevelt/Churchill and the people they respectively led? The outcome was unpredictable in advance and only proven by the actual experiment, with much fear mongering and unexpected consequences along the way. I think Jenkins has it wrong.

Kerry's entire history predicts he will cut and run. The transformational nature of the debates where Kerry suddenly appeared to be a born-again Bushite was typically insincere Kerry at his campaign "finest". As soon as his desired "broader coalition" tells him to get real about Iraq and that they prefer to continue to free-ride on the US' ability to absorb terrorist hits *à la* Clinton (in fact, Kerry is likely to lose allies since Blair will be undermined by a Kerry win and will have no reason to keep his promises to Bush), he will have the reason he needs not to continue Bush's "mistake", which he has no gut interest in proving right. Once elected, Kerry has always proven to be a slacker.

Bush must win in Iraq and the entire Middle-east in order to get the favourable judgement of history he seeks, and, "by God, he will do so". He has been absolutely resolute in his mission since 9/11 and in his ability to carry out a mission since his Christian conversion by Billy Graham in his forties. (Of course, as an economist once parodied that biblical line, "'The race is not always to the swift, or the battle to the strong,' but that is the way to place your bets").

So a Bush win in November should not be a predictor of a quick exit from Iraq (Indeed, the other side would react to that as a defeat since the major objective of the Iraq insurrection has been to defeat democratic US at the polls.

The insurgent Iraqis share this goal with the perfidious French and like-minded Europeans. If Iraq settles out sooner than expected, the next order of business that will justify is to "straighten out" Syria, Iran, and Palestine. A slim but worthy chance. CheerZS

Date: March 9, 2005

From: Zane Spindler
Re: More Jenkins [RS: Refers to Simon Jenkins in *The Times*: **"Let the Middle East sort itself out".]**

"The West would help best by withdrawing its backing from the region's dictators, oil-rich sheikhs and, for that matter, the more extreme elements in Israeli politics. It should leave local popular pressure to do its business its own way, and in its own time. Let Middle Easterners resolve their balance of power their own way, because that way is likely to prove more lasting." Simon Jenkins

That policy worked really well in Rwanda! I am sure the Americans would have been happy to follow this route -- there is little doubt the Israeli's, unrestrained by the US and world opinion, would have set the middle east right many years back. But would that have been acceptable to Jenkins and his ilk? A neutral policy implicitly favours the likely winners -- and whatever they choose to do to win. Would that really be acceptable once the side you favoured did not win? It is futile to complain *ex post*. Jenkins is being disingenuous.

CheerZS

From my diary, 12 April 2005, seminar at Sophia University:

MY SEMINAR AT 5pm went OK. There were about five professors (including Zane and Toshiaki) and 9 or 10 graduate students. I ad libbed on the nature and significance of Currie's "Federal net income-creating expenditure series". I mentioned Alan Sweezy's comment that this was "a semantic triumph of the first magnitude", and Zane later agreed with this but lamented it because it had helped to sell a bad idea – namely, the need for expanded government involvement in the economy. In particular, he condemned the way that private holders of gold were obliged to sell it to the government at the pre-revaluation price. Zane saw this as "confiscation" (or "taking") and an unjust interference with private property rights. To my objection that it was merely a way to prevent the private sector from making an unwarranted windfall gain, Zane replied that it was not a potential windfall but a right vested in holders of gold who had chosen that particular portfolio of assets on the basis of "rational expectations" that were being violated by a corrupt government. I scoffed at this in pointing out to the audience that here was a great example of the divide between the Keynesians and the extreme rational expectations school. Zane objected to my describing it as "extreme". OK, I conceded, it's just the rational expectations view.

Someone else was interested in Currie's attitude to gold, and I explained that he saw it as a major constraint on monetary policy and favoured going off the Gold Standard. I had earlier mentioned that government revenues arising from the revaluation of gold were treated very differently (in assessing its impact on the net income-creating expenditure series) from, say, income tax revenues, because it would have had almost no income-decreasing or private spending effect. Zane disagreed, and he also disagreed, for similar Rational-expectations reasons, to the idea that estate taxes would have very little effect on private spending. I disagreed with him on this too, but conceded that there might be some wealth effect. However, I also insisted that the wealth effect would be of a second order of magnitude compared with the income effect, and that there was relatively little income and expenditure effect arising from measures that curtailed windfall gains from revaluation of gold or the size of inheritances...

Date: 12 April 2005

From: Zane Spindler
Re: Monday's seminar [RS: At Sophia University, Tokyo. Zane was visiting the nearby Seikei University at this point and attended a graduate seminar series at Sophia.]
Hi Roger,

You gave "good seminar" yesterday to quite an interested audience – and they responded in kind.

My comments there were directed more at Currie's paper from which the seminar's title [RS: On Currie's "Federal net income-increasing expenditures series" for the 1930s] was drawn.

It is, of course, remarkable to see such numbers on a monthly basis at that time, well before such figures were regularly constructed as part of the National Accounts, generally on a quarterly basis. But the enterprise, as Sweezy's comment starkly revealed, was mainly a PR exercise. The inclusion or exclusion of any category was not entirely ad hoc, but was nevertheless based on the most casual reasoning, little informed by previous theoretical or empirical work. This is not the judgement of an extreme rational expectations proponent, as you tried to dismiss it, but rather of someone somewhat familiar with the literature prior to Currie's construction of this series.

Consider, for example, David Ricardo, and the Ricardian Equivalence Hypothesis, which suggests that the anticipation of deficit-determined future taxes (legislated taxes to cover debt interest and redemption or inflation taxes associated with excessive monetary creation) would induce equivalent saving. For perfect equivalence, there is no difference in the effects of different methods of financing government expenditure. (For a growing economy, a government could collect and spend the non-inflationary derived seigniorage on its money franchise, but that's it.)

Consider the different conceptions of how government spending should be treated in the national accounts; Kuznets treated government spending on goods and services as part of the final product, Studenski considered it as intermediate product (which, when you look closely at it, seems to be the case). Kuznets' view has prevailed in modern treatments of national accounts, in part, because it validates Keynesian ideas about the various multiplier effects of government spending. With Studenski's approach, government spending on goods and services has the same effect on national income as government transfers, that is, the opposite of the effects of taxes (it's just $Y=C+I+X-M$; not $Y=C+I+G+X-M$). That is, with respect to the product market, the balanced budget multiplier equals zero, and the expenditure multiplier is the same as the tax multiplier but with opposite sign.

Of course, even Keynes, as interpreted by Hansen, would modify product market multipliers by money market interaction, and supply side interaction. Only flat LM & Aggregate Supply curves, special circumstances argued by Keynes, but seldom empirically supported, leave product market multipliers unaffected.

A major oversight of both Keynes, and apparently in this context, Currie, was the supply side effects of various government budget components that actually shift the supply curve for real, not just nominal effects – later this was captured in part by the "real business cycle" theorists, but the Austrians had some theories on this prior to Keynes. Currie was a supply-sider in other contexts, so this oversight might either have been deliberate or inadvertent given his desire to support particular spending policies.

The idea that estate taxes would not affect spending is particularly perverse, both empirically, and from the standpoint of pre-Keynesian and post-Keynesian (but not Post Keynesian) consumption theory and investment theory. It is like the idea, which apparently you support, that government confiscation of private gold holdings would have no adverse expenditure or supply effects. Expectations do not have to be rational, for their confounding to have economic effects. That was one of the key messages of both Keynes' *Treatise on Money* & *General Theory*, although selectively applied.

Imagine how your consumption plans would change if the government decided that St Andrews' properties must be periodically put back into circulation at the market price to new owners, but the original purchase price to previous owners. This is the equivalent of an extra-special tax on such properties (shades of Henry George), which, if it came as a complete surprise, would amount to a reduction in (mortgage-able) wealth on the part of those confiscated (you), with no compensating windfall gain by those who took up the new prices (perhaps, again, you if you still valued it for personal use more than the market). The wealth effect on consumption, especially if applied to properties generally, would be enormous (of course, a balanced budget approach would have to consider what the government did with the proceeds, if actually collected and spent).

However, on these issues, given that you are a dedicated georgist, I am likely preaching to the unconvertible. Nevertheless, there are reasons why Currie's expenditure concept finds less favour today among economists and less import among policy makers.

Like the pump-priming notion, it is a publicity stunt that does not play to modern audiences, who either do not recognise the relevance, or demand a deeper examination and testing of the actual processes.

CheeZS

Diary, 19 April 2005:

ZANE URGES US to visit the controversial Yasukuni shrine which displays a Zero fighter plane that survived. He thinks that an Asian co-prosperity sphere should have been established amicably among all the great powers in the 1920s, with Japan granted trading rights and concessions alongside those established by the British, Americans, Dutch and French.

Diary, 26 April 2005

AT DINNER LAST night after the seminar given by Asahi Noguchi (Senshu University) on Japan's response to the 1930s depression versus their response in the 1990s and early 2000s, Zane gave him a hard time by posing an even more extreme, hard-line Austrian or Tullockian view of the depression: it was the fault of too much discretionary government intervention in the first place, compounded by going off the gold standard and imposing new regulations; and Japan's "deflation" in the 1990s was "good" deflation, or, rather, absence of inflation, and the slow-down in Japan's growth rate merely a symptom of Japan's maturity after post-war reconstruction (artificially boosted by the 1980s credit boom); and the rise in unemployment merely the effect of doing away with featherbedding in order to remain competitive in world markets.

[*EDITORS' NOTE*: AsAHI Noguchi's recollection of that event is found in the next chapter. In this exchange (rapported here by Roger, and later in the recollection from Asahi), the reader will get a glimpse of Zane's intensity and the intellectual *Blitzkriegs* of which he was capable.]

Date: Tue 24/05/2005 06:28

From: Zane Spindler
Re: Vine Rents

"The vine is more affected by the difference of soils than any other fruit tree. From some it derives a flavour which no culture or management can equal, it is supposed, upon any other. This flavour, real or imaginary, is sometimes peculiar to the produce of a few vineyards; sometimes it extends through the greater part of a small district, and sometimes through a considerable part of a large province.

The whole quantity of such wines that is brought to market falls short of the effectual demand, or the demand of those who would be willing to pay the whole rent, profit and wages necessary for preparing and bringing them thither, according to the ordinary rate, or according to the rate at which they are paid in common vineyards. The whole quantity, therefore, can be disposed of to those who are willing to pay more, which necessarily raises the price above that of common wine. The difference is greater or less, according as the fashionableness and scarcity of the wine render the competition of the buyers more or less eager. Whatever it be, the greater part of it goes to the rent of the landlord. For though such vineyards are in general more carefully cultivated than most others, the high price of the wine seems to be, not so much the effect, as the cause of this careful cultivation. In so valuable a produce the loss occasioned by negligence is so great as to force even the most careless to attention. A small part of this high price, therefore, is sufficient to pay the wages of the extraordinary labour bestowed upon their cultivation, and the profits of the extraordinary stock which puts that labour into motion." Adam Smith, Book 1 (*Wealth of Nations*), ch 11 ("Of the rent of land"), paragraph 31.

Date: 23 May 2005

From: Roger Sandilands
Re: Vine rents

This seems an early statement of the Ricardian theory of rent, in which labour gets the same wage whether on favoured or less favoured land, and the difference between one plot's yield and another's goes to the landlord as rent. Rents are high because price is high. Prices are not high because rents are high. Rent is a mere transfer payment for the scarcity value of land that is immobile, fixed in supply, but of varying quality and/or location.

And don't start telling me that it don't exist because of the cost that the besieged landlord must incur to defend it from dissipation. That cost is borne by the exploited taxpayer who finances the police who defend the parasitic landlord class.

CheeHG [RS: Cheers from Henry George]

[This refers to our successful climb up Mount Fuji with Craig Parsons of Yokohama National University]

Date: 25 March 2006 08:30

From: Zane: Spindler
Re: Gabriel Kolko on The Age of War

Roger,

Like many on the left, or in opposition to the US for their own selfish reasons, this fellow spins off half truths and lies into a doomsday scenario.

[This is the first I have heard anyone list Korea as a US failure; it was a political choice not to hold (after taking) the entire peninsula-- a choice likely regretted years later, but hardly a failure, when considering the South's fifty years of relative prosperity compared with the North's impoverishment. That Russia is no longer a potential balance to the US, with all its nukes and large standing army, another wishful fiction -- especially with Putin at the helm. This guy is what supposedly Lenin called "a useful idiot".]

These people should ask themselves who will be in a position to credibly restrain the opportunistic dictators if the US loses either its will or credibility (by quitting early) to project force in opposition. Of course, many, and this chap sounds like one of them, would wish for that outcome because they are consciously or unconsciously shills for such dictators. (The record of how many in the media, like politicians in France and Russia, were in on Saddam's Oil for Food scam, has not yet been raised by the media, but of course that would not be a conspiracy would it?) Maintaining a "Fortress America" in the 1940s and onwards would have left you a citizen of the Third Reich!

The US's record of successes is matched by a record of failures only when they have prematurely lost the will to continue; they were psychologically defeated by people just like this guy both inside and out. But they have had successes when they went for, and paid the cost for, unconditional surrender and re-constituting the offending societies as in Germany and Japan.

How many people now would wish that the US had not done that? Maybe those who do not well remember what was done, or those who might have spun out an alternative success story (as I was doing last year with the speculation that the US might have benefited more by letting the Japanese give non-communistic order to East Asia).

Currently, there seems to be an excessive concern with the cost of the Iraq war without regard to the cost to the US of not finishing that war successfully -- or to the cost to world order.

Think of all the cases over the last decade where the US did not intervene, because there was no domestic or international consensus for it to do so -- Rwanda, Bosnia (until it was too late), Darfur, etc. -- or places where political pressure backed by a realistic threat of military deployment could affect beneficial change -- Zimbabwe, Cuba, Venezuela, etc. -- if the world community could get on side.

Think of what will happen to the globalization of economic activity which is only now recovering from the breakdown in international security provided by the British Navy prior to their own loss of will to maintain a 2 to 1 ratio in capital ships.

This guy also seems to forget that during WWII the US was able to fight a two-front war and devote 50% of its (much smaller) economy to that effort, and to incur casualties that were a high multiple of anything incurred since.

I guess if people like him can fool the American people into thinking they have no ability or interest in participating in providing world order, it will be a self-fulfilling prophecy -- and that may well cost more than they can possibly imagine.

Part of their strategy is to smear the US as an "evil empire".

But once you have placed your bets on "soft power" like Canada, even a tiny country like Denmark can take your territory without fear of meaningful reprisals -- as Canadians are just now learning.

See below:

[Speak Softly and Carry a Smaller Stick, by Andrew Kohut, March 24, 2006, *NY Times*]

CheerZS

Date: 09 November 2006 07:23

From: Zane Spindler
Re: Fancy Nancy?

I think Rumsfeld has been an extremely competent Defence Secretary, who became a "stalking horse" for those opposed to the Iraq War *per se*, not just the way it was prosecuted. He will now serve Bush well by being a "sacrificial lamb."

If others had served Bush as well, Bush would have accomplished more (The Republican Majority in both Houses did not serve Bush well over these last two years thereby dissipating his mandate from the 2004 election with which he had hoped to do much more. Bush may be more successful with the new, more bipartisan Congress -- which does not represent the success the Democrats expected, so their new mandate is moderated).

What I will miss is Rumsfeld's handling of the press, which was better high comedy than The Daily Show. Just like Bush's first press secretary, Ari Fleischer, who was way too clever for the press, and was generally able to make them sound foolish and childish in their whiny ways.

It is now common for even Rumsfeld's supporters to admit he made mistakes, just as it is now common for NeoCons to reportedly admit mistakes were made in prosecuting the war.

However, I think in war, the biggest mistake is always to be distracted from winning by quibbling over mistakes. An enemy's best strategy is always to provoke that diversion if possible and here the foreign enemy has been aided by domestic enemies of Bush.

Whatever is done will be a "mistake" if the enemy makes better use of it. Should the Iraqi Army have been disbanded?

There were pros and cons discussed in the press at the time and the consensus supported the decision taken -- but now that is regarded as Rumsfeld's mistake. Perhaps it was, if the press had any influence on him or the President. [As Trotsky determined with the Red Army, democracy was no way to run it]. Whatever was done with the Iraqi Army would be problematic, and, hence, in retrospect, a mistake.

The ultimate objectives in Iraq have never been those that an army or the Defence Department could accomplish by itself (At least with both arms tied behind its back in order to make it comply with liberal enlightened ideas about how the US image should be presented and preserved -- now there is a big mistake), and the other agencies in the US Government have not been on side or particularly competent in meeting those goals.

Still, it must be admitted that the situation is not static but dynamic with a determined internal and external opposition against settling the conflict according to a US timetable.

That will still be the case after Rumsfeld, and if US & Washington remains divided on this issue, one cannot expect that things will improve to the satisfaction of US Congress, US voters, or US media. As Rumsfeld observed, the war will be won or lost in Washington. Without him, it will be more likely to be lost. But that will seem like a "win" to those who never favoured it.

And Nancy was Nancy Pelosi. Not that I know much about her either (though I believe she has a reputation as a leftist?); but whereas (this is the brainless sexist in me) I can't abide Hillary to look at or listen to, she is not a "babe" (who would appeal to our baser instincts) but rather a "matron" -- very much like an "elephant matriarch" who is in charge of the herd's well-being (an apt analogy given she started out as a Republican). Her greatest accomplishment so far is to keep her family's political capital intact and growing.

She is a better looking, anti-war, pro-gay version of Thatcher, who I gather you didn't like because she was lacking those more frivolous sentiments. ;---)

The Henry George Chair

HENRY GEORGE WAS a personage of fascination to Zane. My "Henry George Chair" was, if not a touchstone then a pleasant backdrop to our debates. Its provenance is well documented. It was presented to a Peter Burt, JP, a Glasgow Liberal councillor who played a leading role in persuading Lloyd George to introduce a land tax bill in his 1909 "People's Budget". This was blocked by the House of Lords, which in turn led to their power to interfere with finance bills being abolished in 1911. I bought it at an auction about 30 years ago and kept in my university office where it gave me many opportunities to proselitise on behalf of Henry George! The caption reads 'Free Land, Free Trade, Free Men. Tax Land Values.' I used to say that I was the only person in the UK with a real chair of economics.

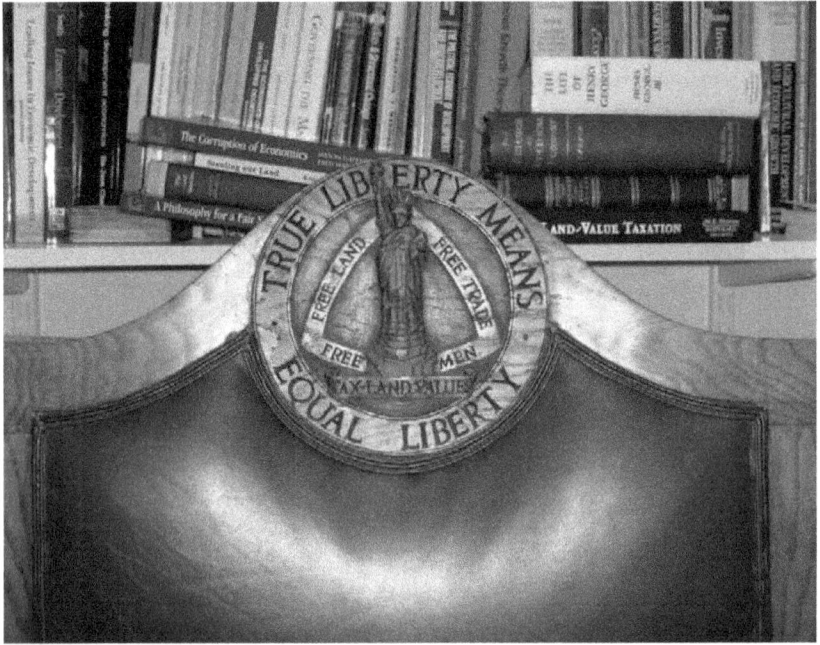

RAINMAKER 7

ASAHI NOGUCHI AND ZANE SPINDLER

*Z*ANE HELPED MANY A YOUNG economist along in his or her careers. In this chapter you get a glimpse of Zane writing a detailed letter of support for a research prize that Filip Palda was applying for at his school. You also see Zane trying to recruit to his particular view of economic methodology Asahi Noguchi.

In the following section entitled "How Should An Economic Policy making Be Analyzed and Evaluated?" Professor Noguchi explains the intensity which Zane could bring to ensuring that a fellow economist was on the right mental path. In the section that follows one sees the effort Zane could put into making sure a fellow economist was on the right path. Both sections show Zane acting as a catalyst for the intellectual progress of economics. A true rainmaker of the profession.

Asahi Noguchi's essay on Zane

I MET ZANE Spindler on April 25th 2005, which is the date I delivered my presentation at Sophia University, Tokyo. The title of my talk was "The Role of Misguided Economic Ideas in Macroeconomic Policy Making: Japan's Experiences in the Two Deflationary Periods." It was presented as one of a seminar series on the history of economic theory and economic policy, which had been hosted jointly by Toshiaki Hirai, then a professor at Sophia University, and Roger Sandilands, then a visiting professor at Sophia University. Most of the regular participants and presenters were scholars or graduate students. Among them was Zane, who was in Japan as a visiting fellow at Seikei University, Tokyo, at that time. Zane also made his own presentation entitled "A Public Choice Perspective on the Origins of the Pacific War" on some date after mine, which I could not attend. Actually my participation in this joint seminar was confined to my April 25th presentation, so that face-to-face communication between Zane and me was done only at this occasion, specifically within the seminar discussion and the dinner after the seminar. This means most of intellectual interrelation between Zane and me was constructed on e-mail interchange between us. With the help of Roger Sandilands, here I selected the e-mails in which Zane and I were arguing about economic policy-making, the subject that both of us had been investigating from quite contrasting viewpoints.

The contents of my April 25th presentation was based on a research that I had been conducting jointly with Koichi Hamada, then a professor at Yale. The research was mostly done during April 2003 and March 2004, while I was a visiting fellow at Yale. Prior to my presentation, I asked Professor Hirai, the organizer, to deliver our paper that had been already circulated as a discussion paper (Hamada and Noguchi, 2005a). Thus it should be noted that "the paper" to which Zane referred in the e-mails was actually this one. Since this paper contained vast citations from historical documents, we truncated its citation part when it was finally published (Hamada and Noguchi, 2005b). The general purpose of our research would not be comprehensible with the following abstract.

This paper examines the role of misleading economic ideas that most likely promoted the economic disasters of the two deflationary periods in Japanese economic history. Misleading ideas deepened the depression during the interwar years, and erroneous thinking has prolonged the stagnation of the Japanese economy since the 1990s. While the current framework of political economy is based on the self-interest of political agents as well as that of voters, we highlight the role of ideas in policy making, in particular, in the field of macroeconomics where the incidence of a particular policy is not clear to the public. Using two significant examples, this paper illustrates the role of preconceived ideas, in contrast to economic interests, as dominant forces influencing economic policy making.

During the seminar discussion and at the dinner, Zane was making a strong argument against us, which is nicely summarized in Professor Sandilands' diary of 26th April 2005.

> At dinner last night after the seminar given by Asahi Noguchi (Senshu University) on Japan's response to the 1930s depression versus their response in the 1990s and early 2000s, Zane gave him a hard time by posing an even more extreme, hard-line Austrian or Tullockian view of the depression: it was the fault of too much discretionary government intervention in the first place, compounded by going off the Gold Standard and imposing new regulations; and Japan's "deflation" in the 1990s was "good" deflation, or, rather, absence of inflation, and the slow-down in Japan's growth rate merely a symptom of Japan's maturity after post-war reconstruction (artificially boosted by the 1980s credit boom); and the rise in unemployment merely the effect of doing away with featherbedding in order to remain competitive in world markets.

When I began to communicate with Zane via e-mails, I thought he was mainly criticizing the approach we adopted for analyzing economic policy making. In our paper, we took what Mark Blaug designated as an "absolutist" approach

(Blaug, 1962), in which economic policy making is to be evaluated with some definite criterion. We knew that it might be quite problematic to set such a criterion. We dared to do this nevertheless. At first I thought that Zane was taking a "relativist" approach that places more importance on an analysis of the various motives for economic policy making than for evaluating the policy. However, I immediately came to know that the difference between Zane and me was more profound. We had quite different notions about how economic policy should be formulated. It seemed to me that Zane distrusted public policy in general. We also had quite different views on what kind of economic reasoning was right or wrong, which was revealed most distinctly through our arguments on Friedrich Hayek, specifically on his policy stance during the two World Wars which Hayek himself mentioned in his Alfred Nobel Memorial Lecture delivered on 11 December, 1974, at the Stockholm School of Economics (Hayek, 1975). In the e-mail debate with Zane, I referred to the transcription of Hayek's Nobel Lecture I found on the Internet.

The debate between Zane and me initially started as a private exchange of e-mails. From April 27th to May 4th 2005, there were numerous e-mail correspondences between the two of us. The first email from Zane set the tone for our exchange. In the middle of the actual exchanges, I thought that I had better make our debate open to other participants of the seminar. Professor Hirai had already arranged a mailing list named "jointseminar" aimed mainly to deliver notices for the seminar members. I thought we could utilize this mailing list as a place for post-seminar discussion with all the participants. So I proposed to Zane that we should move to this mailing list. Zane approved it at once. I put forward all of our previous e-mail correspondences to the "jointseminar" list, so that the other members could easily catch up with our arguments. Masazumi Wakatabe, who was one of the members and was to make his own presentation titled "Was the Great Depression the Watershed of Macroeconomics?: The Impact of the Great Depression on Economic Thought Reconsidered," immediately offered his comments. I also collected all of the related discussion posted to the "jointseminar" mailing list, up to Professor Wakatabe's last entry of May 18th [*Editors' note*: unfortunately due to space constraints and the complexity of the email debate with a third party joining, and the ensuing tangled references to all that had followed, Professor Wakatabe's contribution has been left out].

I still remember an unusual tension that I felt while I was arguing with Zane. We might have scarcely attained agreement no matter how long we continued our argument. Nevertheless I greatly regret that I have lost a chance to reopen the debate with Zane forever. Since the time of our exchanges, the global economy has experienced one of the greatest economic debacles. Countries all over the world then set out unprecedented macroeconomic policies that no one could ever have imagined. I greatly wish I could hear what Zane would have argued about the situation.

References

Blaug, Mark (1962) *Economic Theory in Retrospect*, Illinois: Richard D. Irwin, Homewood.

Hamada, Koichi and Asahi Noguchi (2005a) "The Role of Preconceived Ideas in Macroeconomic Policy: Japan's Experiences in the Two Deflationary Periods," Center Discussion Paper, No.908, March 2005, Economic Growth Center, Yale University (http://www.econ.yale.edu/growth_pdf/cdp908.pdf).

Hamada, Koichi and Asahi Noguchi (2005b) "The Role of Preconceived Ideas in Macroeconomic Policy: Japan's Experiences in the Two Deflationary Periods," *International Economics and Economic Policy*. 2:101-126.

Hayek, Friedrich (1975) *Full Employment at Any Price?*, London: Institute of Economic Affairs.

Email correspondence between Asahi Noguchi and Zane

Date: 27 Apr 2005
To: Asahi Noguchi
From: Zane Spindler
Subject: Post-Seminar Economics 1, Zane->Asahi
Hi Asahi,

As I said, I liked your paper very much for its methodology, which I think can be quite revealing to those who think policy-making is only a matter of optimizing by a benevolent policy-maker. Personally, I would hesitate to make definitive arguments about one or another policy being "erroneous", which at best, is even contentious in retrospect, and then even many years afterwards as history is continually rewritten in light of newly emerging theories. Rather, I would advise concentrating on the implications of the Kydland and Prescott perspective when the political competition between special-interest, political pressure groups, with differing theories of economic structure and public policies, create macro-economic coordination difficulties as public and private agents are basing their behaviour on differently formed expectations and beliefs which, without a spontaneous coordinating mechanism, are likely to be, and to remain, inconsistent.

In the democratic context, a non-erroneous policy would be one that simultaneously coordinates all agents' beliefs, expectations, preferences and plans to converge consistently and quickly to a path consistent with the underlying physical, technical and institutional reality. Unfortunately, as Hayek has argued, the requisite knowledge is unavailable for formulating such ongoing policies. Their implementation in modern democracies is also problematic, as is even the implementation and maintenance of longer run policies of establishing credible institutions, such as the Gold Standard or zero-inflation rate targeting, cyclically-balanced budgets, etc.

Of course, there would be little for economists to do if this were not the case. As it is, there is plenty for us to do arguing about which of our policies are less erroneous on behalf of contending special interests, including, most importantly, our own.

CheerZS

Zane

Date: 29 Apr 2005
To: Zane Spindler
From: Asahi Noguchi
Subject: Post-Seminar Economics 2, Asahi->Zane
Dear Zane,

Thanks again for your comments. They are quite helpful because they would force us to refine our arguments.

I am pleased to know that you are favourable to our approach emphasizing the importance of ideas rather than economic interests. Once we were told by a political scientist that an idea-based approach is "without micro-foundation." One purpose of our paper is to argue that this is not the case.

As to policy episodes,

I suppose that a difference between us might be how we should utilize our economic knowledge. I believe in the Popperian view that progress in scientific theories is a replacement of one theory, which is less erroneous, for the other. This is a continuous and never-ending process, so that today's theory would necessarily be replaced by another theory in the future. In the sphere of policy-making, however, we can't rely on a future theory that would certainly be better and less erroneous. We are always forced to choose a certain policy among many alternatives. All what we can do then is to make use of the best available knowledge at the time. Similarly, we should evaluate past economic policies from the best available knowledge now. The evaluation would change as a theoretical framework itself changes. I think we should do this nevertheless, since these historical experiences would not provide any lessons without these evaluations.

I am sure we have another chance to argue, and looking forward to it.

Sincerely,
Asahi

Date: 29 Apr 2005
To: Asahi Noguchi
From: Zane Spindler
Subject: Post-Seminar Economics 3, Zane->Asahi
Hi Asahi,
You wrote

> I am pleased to know that you are favourable to our approach emphasizing the importance of ideas rather than economic interests. Once we were told by a political scientist that an idea-based approach is "without micro-foundation." One purpose of our paper is to argue that this is not the case.

The question for that political scientist is: "Where do ideas come from?" Especially: "Where do ideas about the general interest come from?" Like all public policies (which are public goods or bads, which in turn are supposedly under-provided by private interests... as is governance, so governance is also under-provided -- and then only by private interests. As an infinite regress, you can see where this gets one), general interest ideas are public goods which are provided privately to serve private interests in the name of general interests (The public choice perspective).

This is no less true of general interest ideas provided (privately) by economists. Keynes, you may recall had a very specific private interest he was pursuing in providing his *General Theory* and all his other theories. His ambition was to direct the economic policy of the British (and, perhaps later on, the World) government.

You also wrote "As to policy episodes, I suppose that a difference between us might be how we should utilize our economic knowledge." True. I think we should be very careful because someday, like architects, we may be held liable for the damage done when our models fail. (George Stigler had a very funny "miscellany" article on this in *JPE* in the early 70s, reprinted in his book *The Economist as Preacher*, and entitled: "A short sketch of the history of truth in teaching economics". One of his conclusions was that economic development would be dropped as a university discipline because no university could afford to settle a suit for the damages done by developmental economists!)

You wrote

I believe in the Popperian view that progress in scientific theories is a replacement of one theory, which is less erroneous, for the other.

> This is a continuous and never-ending process, so that today's the-
> ory would necessarily be replaced by another theory in the future.

That's a likely story. And believable as far as it goes. But there is no mechanism that guarantees less erroneous theories survive this evolutionary process, just as there is no mechanism that guarantees that natural selection will always produce the fittest species for all unforeseen and, as yet, unexperienced future conditions. Indeed, if we look at the evolution of theories in economics, and even the hard sciences, we see hoaxes and fads lasting for considerable periods of time, during which their application leads to substantial misallocation and maldistribution. Peer review, promotion/tenure, and granting systems do not always provide a useful screening method, as is sometimes asserted, because they are often based on erroneous theories or successful fads of the past and present, to say nothing of the professional and unprofessional jealousies that are all too important in the short run. Incidentally, by accepting Popper's view one is admitting that one's policy advice is likely based on error. Without a disclaimer to that effect, one is liable; with such a disclaimer one loses credibility.

You wrote "In the sphere of policy-making, however, we can't rely on a future theory that would certainly be better and less erroneous." Not "certainly" as I have argued above. We are always forced to choose a certain policy among many alternatives. Who is "forcing" us to do this? Isn't it a matter of choice and free will? We may or may not choose to advise and consult in return for fortune and fame -- though it may turn out to be for damages and infamy -- we are not without examples of the latter. However, given the 20th century notion that the government is responsible for economic stabilization and growth, Pandora's box has already been opened. As a practical matter, someone (even many) will step forward to advise poli-cy -- and others will criticize those policies. This ongoing pro-cess (which is what you are analysing in your paper) will create a presumptuous "conventional wisdom" which may, at times, be at odds with (perhaps an equally presumptuous) "conven-tional theory". Proponents of each will judge the proponents of the other to be in error.

Does your paper really gain by taking sides? As you write "All what we can do then is to make use of the best available knowledge at the time." But as Hayek believably argued, no single individual planner or policy maker has such knowl-edge. Further, a consensus of professionals is also an inad-equate basis for a "knowledge consensus" because it is not weighted by the relative importance of what each knows, as is the case with people who actually trade in markets based on their knowledge and have something personal at stake other than their reputations.

You write that

> Similarly, we should evaluate past economic policies from the best available knowledge now. The evaluation would change as a theo-retical framework itself changes. I think we should do this never-theless, since these historical experiences would not provide any lessons without these evaluations.

Here I agree totally, but this is generally not done in economics as it is in hard sciences, and even when it is done, it is seldom given the attention it deserves. Consider how economic histo-ry has fallen into disfavour at many major US graduate schools. One useful attempt at evaluating policy is: *What's Economics Worth: Valuing Policy Research*. Ed. P.G. Pardey & V.H. Smith. Johns Hopkins 2004.

You write "I am sure we have another chance to argue, and looking forward to it." Right! An exciting prospect.

CheerZS

Zane

Date: 2 May 2005
To: Zane Spindler
From: Asahi Noguchi
Subject: Post-Seminar Economics 4, Asahi->Zane

Dear Zane,

I appreciate your arguments. I generally agree with them, at least individually. I agree with your thesis that general interest ideas as public goods tend to be under-provided, an existing theory may turn out to be false someday, hoaxes and fads rather than less erroneous theories would last for considerable periods of time, and so forth.

Your arguments reaffirmed for me however that we have quite different views on the role of economics. It seems to me that you are sceptical to economic policies in general. I admit economics is basically a tool for understanding economic phenomena. It doesn't have to be useful in a material sense. It can continue to be a discipline of genuine academic interest such as archaeology.

Unfortunately, it is not as such. Actually, economics has absorbed human and other resources far larger than can be justifiable for merely an academic interest. It has done so because our society believes economic knowledge can applicable to solve many economic problems facing it, thus to enhance its economic welfare. It is exactly what society expects for the economic profession.

I think most of the greatest economists, *e.g.*, Smith, Ricardo, Keynes, etc., had successfully done this task. I don't believe the world without Smith and Ricardo would had been better than the one with them. In their day "free trade" had been an intentional economic policy that was meant to destroy existing economic orders and systems. Even policy sceptics such as Hayek, not to mention Keynes, were not free from policy commitment. In fact, Hayek advised people not to use expansionary monetary policy in the time of the Great Depression saying that it would make the matter worse. Apparently he was advocating a policy on this occasion. And it is a policy that Hayek himself later admitted to be wrong.

I completely agree with you in that, as you write "We may or may not choose to advise and consult in return for fortune and fame -- though it may turn out to be for damages and infamy -- we are not without examples of the latter." Hayek and Lionel Robbins have been criticized later for their wrong policy advice during the Great Depression. However, I don't think they shouldn't have told anything about policy. Actually, their failure greatly contributed to our economic understanding that the reverse is the case, *i.e.*, a quite aggressive monetary policy would be necessitated at these occasions. As this story shows, every policy advice has a risk for infamy. I think it is something inescapable, however.

I also agree with you saying that

> As a practical matter, someone (even many) will step forward to advise policy -- and others will criticize those policies. This ongoing process (which is what you are analysing in your paper) will create a presumptuous "conventional wisdom" which may at times be at odds with (perhaps an equally presumptuous) "conventional theory". Proponents of each will judge the proponents of the other to be in error."

That is what a science is all about. As Popper argued, a positive science is a continuous process of beating conventional theory by the other. If there were two competing hypotheses which intend to explain a same phenomenon, the one would turn out to be less erroneous than the other from empirical grounds. The scientists in both camps, the old and the new, usually endeavor to defend their positions and attack the opponents. If it were ever a positive science, however, the battle would lead to a conclusion eventually. Though I admit that economics is quite an obscure and impure science, I think this picture roughly holds for economics.

Sincerely, Asahi

Date: 2 May 2005
To: Asahi Noguchi
From: Zane Spindler
Subject: Post-Seminar Economics 5, Zane->Asahi
Hi Asahi,
You wrote

> I appreciate your arguments. I generally agree with them, at least individually. I agree with your theses that the general interest ideas as public goods tend to be under-provided, an existing theory may turn out to be false someday, hoaxes and fads rather than less erroneous theories would last for considerable periods of time, and so forth. Your arguments reaffirmed me, however, that we have quite different views on the role of economics. It seems to me that you are skeptical to economic policies in general.

The finer the tuning, the more skeptical are most economists these days, though perhaps that is not the case at some notable schools most closely connected to the "Beltway". The

consensus I see seems to favour policies with respect to institutional forms -- that is, constitutional political economy --
which aims at providing relative certainty about the nature
and range of government actions. In part, this addresses the
Kydland and Prescott problem, and it simplifies private agents'
learning from their own economic "experiments" testing their
own "theories" *à la* Popper.

You also wrote

> I admit economics is basically a tool for understanding economic
> phenomena. It doesn't have to be useful in a material sense. It can
> continue to be a discipline of genuine academic interest such as
> archaeology. Unfortunately, it is not as such. Actually, economics
> has absorbed human and other resources far larger than can be
> justifiable for merely an academic interest.

That probably applies to many other social sciences and the
humanities as well... luckily for those fields participants. You
go on "It is because our society believe economic knowledge
can applicable to solve many economic problems facing it, thus
to enhance its economic welfare. It is exactly what the society expects for the economic profession." Who or what is this
"society" to which you are attributing such expectations? It
seems to me that some economists would like to believe such
an idea, but the reality is that as individuals, economists sell
their ideas to their consumers, as individuals and as institutions, just like other merchants, and their consumers expect
some product quality to be delivered or they won't be repeat
buyers. Those in the media and in politics may benefit by promoting the idea that government can and should solve individuals' problems, and the politicians in turn may hire in-
house economists (bureaucrats), and contract-out to freelance

economists, to obtain (often contradictory) advice -- the main effect of which is to solve economists' income and self-employment problems and to co-opt potential government critics.

Now this is perhaps also a remaining difference between us, because, so far in our exchanges, you have not explicitly acknowledged the role of economists' self-interest in their own policy advising. This is not inconsequential because I think your paper could be considerably strengthened by your addressing this issue in it explicitly. You wrote "I think most of the greatest economists, *e.g.*, Smith, Ricardo, Keynes, etc., had successfully done this task. I don't believe a world without Smith and Ricardo would have been better than the one with them." As somewhat mainstream economists, we might be prejudiced on that matter. Do you feel the same way about Marx, for example?

You wrote

> At their times, "free trade" had been an intentional economic policy that meant to destroy existing economic orders and systems. Even policy skeptics such as Hayek, not to mention Keynes, were not free from policy commitment. In fact, Hayek advised the people not to use expansionary monetary policy in the time of the Great Depression saying that it would make the matter worse. Apparently he was saying a policy at this occasion. And it is the policy that Hayek himself later admitted to be wrong.

I would like to see that citation. What I remember is Hayek admitting Keynes was wrong!!!! At any rate, Hayek, as an Austrian, was talking about stabilizing monetary institutions so as not to have the seeds of the next depression sown in an excessive over-expansion in the preceding boom. This is a constitutional perspective.

As I said at your paper presentation, reintroducing the Gold Standard was not the original error, but rather dropping it in the first place. Had all countries played by the Gold Standard rules consistently, the events of the first half of the 20th century would have played out much differently especially with respect to hot wars and trade wars. Similarly for Japan in the 90s, where previously excessive and unsustainable credit and monetary [expansion] had set the scene from which there was no easy exit. We may or may not choose to advise and consult in return for fortune and fame -- though it may turn out to be for damages and infamy -- we are not without examples of the latter.

You wrote

> Hayek and Lionel Robbins have been criticized later for their wrong policy advice during the Great Depression. However, I don't think they shouldn't have told anything about policy. Actually, their failure greatly contributed to our economic understanding that the reverse is the case, *i.e.*, a quite aggressive monetary policy would be necessitated at these occasions. As this story shows, every policy advice has a risk for infamy. I think it is something inescapable, however.

It may well be an error to think Hayek and Robbins in error. It was not necessarily Keynesian economics that saved the day toward the end of the 30s, but rather what few economists recognize as "Orwellian economics" (after George Orwell in *1984*). Hot war and then cold war saved advanced economies the fate such economies experienced post WWI. When "peace threatened to break out" after the fall of the Berlin Wall and then the fall of the USSR, some economies came to grief faster than others as a result of necessary restructuring, but the re-invigorated "War on Terror" may now help revive some and maintain others well into the foreseeable future. As a practical matter, someone (even many) will step forward to advise policy -- and others will criticize those policies. This ongoing process (which is what you are analysing in your paper) will create a presumptuous "conventional wisdom" which may at times be at odds with (perhaps an equally presumptuous) "conventional theory". Proponents of each will judge the proponents of the other to be in error.

You wrote

> That is what a science is all about. As Popper argued, a positive science is a continuous process of beating conventional theory by the other. If there were two competitive hypotheses which intend to explain a same phenomenon, the one would turn out to be less erroneous than the other from empirical grounds. The scientists in both camps, the old and the new, usually endeavor to defend their positions and attack the opponents. If it were ever a positive science, however, the battle would lead to a conclusion eventually. Though I admit that economics is quite an obscure and impure science, I think this picture roughly holds for economics.

Well, the test of that is whether economists are really willing to do what they (you) say -- or whether that is just so much rhetoric (to refer to a classic article on that very issue which shows that in general economists do not do as they say). We can see many instances where observation and evidence might suggest one solution is better than another, and yet it is not the one chosen by economists because it is not in their interest to do so. A case in point is the central bank. Most evidence gathered so far is that most economies that have introduced central banks during the 20th century have not done as well as those that do not have central banks.

Yet most economists are not only not aware of this evidence, they typically refuse to accept it. They refuse to give up their professional "lottery ticket" for a share of the presumed seigniorage.

I think that your article would be better if the role of interests in the creation and competition of economic ideas was made the central focus, rather than which idea/policy was or was not in error -- the latter is a never ending debate. Further, it might not be best as a publication strategy since potential referees may not agree with your judgement as to who was in error.

CheerZS

Zane

Date: 3 May 2005
To: Zane Spindler
From: Asahi Noguchi
Subject: Post-Seminar Economics 6, Asahi->Zane
Dear Zane,

I will try to make my response as concise as possible. It is only to make clear some subtle points.

You wrote

The finer the tuning, the more skeptical are most economists these days, though perhaps that is not the case at some notable schools most closely connected to the "Beltway". The consensus I see seems to favour policies with respect to institutional forms -- that is, constitutional political economy -- which aims at providing relative certainty about the nature and range of government actions. In part, this addresses the Kydland and Prescott problem, and it simplifies private agents' learning from their own economic "experiments" testing their own "theories" *à la* Popper.

I don't oppose it. By saying a policy, I don't mean old-Keynesian way of macro-economic fine tuning which was prevalent several decades ago. I believe most of the economists in this field have well recognized, partly thanks to Kydland and Prescott, the importance of policy rules or commitments on the side of governments or central banks. In my view, this is one good example of Popperian scientific evolution, since it apparently shows that our economic knowledge, and policy prescription based on it, is becoming less and less erroneous. It is because our society believes economic knowledge can solve many economic problems facing it and thus enhance its economic welfare. It is exactly what society expects for the economic profession.

You wrote

Who or what is this "society" to which you are attributing such expectations? It seems to me that some economists would like to believe such an idea, but the reality is that as individuals, economists sell their ideas to their consumers, as individuals and as institutions, just like other merchants, and their consumers expect some product quality to be delivered or they won't be repeat buyers. Those in the media and in politics may benefit by promoting the idea that government can and should solve individuals' problems, and the politicians in turn may hire in-house economists (bureaucrats), and contract-out to freelance economists, to obtain (often contradictory) advice -- the main effect of which is to solve economists' income and self-employment problems and to co-opt potential government critics.

In a broader sense, all scientists, not to mention economists, are selling their ideas, that is making their own living by doing some research activities and publishing their results. There is no other way that the scientists can be useful in the society, although some of them might be useless or even harmful.

I appreciate your advice. It is likely that we must be determined to encounter many debates as long as we hold to our own criterion of good and bad economics.

Sincerely,

Asahi

Date: 3 May 2005
To: Asahi Noguchi
From: Zane Spindler
Subject: Post-Seminar Economics 7, Zane->Asahi

Hi Asahi,

You wrote that "Here Hayek is saying reluctantly that Keynes was right and he was wrong, at least as to the policy prescription during the inter-war period". A close reading does not support your interpretation. Hayek is saying that Keynes was wrong, in introducing Keynes' version of what Hayek refers to as the "fatal conceit"; Hayek does not admit he (Hayek) was wrong about the economics he supported (the Gold Standard, but not at the previous exchange rate) but rather that he (Hayek) was wrong about the politics during the 30s -- about the feasibility of pursuing an appropriate policy in the face of special interest political opposition organized around a general interest idea -- fatally attractive as the case may be -- put forwarded and supposedly rationalized by Keynes' *General Theory*. Others had put forward similar proposals for government interventions (even Pigou, as a more politically realistic alternative to a general fall in wages, and my old pal, Lauchlin Currie, the drafter of the 1935 Federal Reserve Act and first economic advisor to a US President), but Keynes had enticed younger economists (and subsequently, the general population of the economically literate) into acts of faith based on the *General Theory*, which played to and strengthened the special interests clamouring for changes in government policy during the 30s. Nevertheless, these policies were not a clear success during the mid-to-late 30s; the US economy fully revived only once war preparations were well underway.

You wrote "I appreciate your advice. It is likely that we must be determined to encounter many debates as long as we hold to our own criterion of good and bad economics." Here is a way to finesse the issue. Consider the competition of ideas to be like a war where the "winners" get to write the "history" -- which in this case, means determining who was in "error". That way you are not opening a debate, but considering it closed as a result of past interactions.

Another important point is that a public debate over policy issues can serve a coordination function when there is a clear winner that convinces most economic agents of the appropriateness of a given policy such that they make their decisions based on that policy and the belief in the policy's consequences -- of course, in order for this to achieve a genuine coordination, the policy must be consistent with reality and with expectations based on it.

CheerZS
Zane

Date: 4 May 2005
To: Zane Spindler
From: Asahi Noguchi
Subject: Post-Seminar Economics 8, Asahi->Zane

Dear Zane,

It might be an exaggeration to say that Hayek admitted Keynes was right, because his hatred toward Keynes is apparent in every aspect. I also accept your general interpretation behind the issue. I still think, however, my interpretation is proper in that Hayek admitted his mistake on his policy position during the period.

Hayek said that

> I have to confess that 40 years ago I argued differently. I have since altered my opinion -- not about the theoretical explanation of the events but about the practical possibility of removing the obstacles to the functioning of the system by allowing deflation to proceed for a while. I then believed that a short process of deflation might break the rigidity of money wages (what economists have since come to call their 'rigidity downwards') or the resistance to the reduction of some particular money wages, and that in this way we could restore relative wages determined by the market. This seems to me still an indispensable condition if the market mechanism is to function satisfactorily. But I no longer believe it is in practice possible to achieve it in this manner. I probably should have seen then that the last chance was lost after the British government in 1931 abandoned the attempt to bring costs down by deflation just when it seemed near success.

A literal reading of these passages tells us: 40 years ago (from the year 1974) Hayek thought that a process of deflation was necessary because it might break the rigidity of money wages and restore relative wages determined by the market, but Hayek in the year 1974 no longer believes it is in practice possible to achieve it in this manner, which means Hayek admitted his misjudgment in the former period. We know that an idea of intentional deflation for the purpose of breaking the rigidity of money wages was what Keynes attacked most relentlessly. Therefore we can logically conclude that Hayek virtually admitted Keynes was right, although Hayek would never admit it by himself.

You wrote

> Another important point is that a public debate over policy issues can serve a coordination function when there is a clear winner that convinces most economic agents of the appropriateness of a given policy such that they make their decisions based on that policy and the belief in the policy's consequences -- of course, in order for this to achieve a genuine coordination, the policy must be consistent with reality and with expectations based on it.

This is exactly the reason why we focus on the role of ideas. Suppose that there is some winning policy idea, or preoccupied idea in our terminology, that has successfully convinced most economic agents. As long as this conventional idea is consistent, at least roughly, with reality, preoccupation would do no harm. Rather, it would minimize a cost of social consent. A problem would occur when the conventional idea is inconsistent with reality in some fatal aspects. We think we are dealing with these cases.

Sincerely,
Asahi

Date: 4 May 2005
To: Asahi Noguchi
From: Zane Spindler
Subject: Post-Seminar Economics 9, Zane->Asahi
Dear Asahi,

I think the way to look at those passages is that Hayek recognized that he, and others like him, were "steamrollered" politically by the "Keynesian revolution", which gave an exciting general interest rationale for special interest lobbying and for politicians trying to exploit a new "policy niche". Hayek thought that Keynes' general interest rationale was wrong because it created expectations which would have inflationary consequences, but he admitted he lost the debate. He then set out to counter the Keynesian Revolution by writing books like *The Road to Serfdom, The Fatal Conceit, The Denationalization of Money*, and many others putting forward a constitutional political economy perspective. He made clear in that passage that his support of the Gold Standard being reintroduced was not at the previous price, citing Ricardo as an authority on this issue. To interpret this passage as Hayek saying his (Hayek's) economics was wrong is akin to those who photo-shopped the photo of Bush reading a children's book to make it look like the book was upside down. There are still people who believe that altered Bush photo was a genuine original just as there are people who will always believe that Hayek was saying he was wrong on policy during the 30s, rather than that he had not won on policy during the 30s. Big difference!

Incidentally, if you read Roger Sandilands' book on Lauchlin Currie, you will see that those who were trying to apply Keynesian style policies, like Lauchlin, experienced as many disappointments as successes -- and they were constantly concerned with choosing the most favourable language with which to sell those policies. Thus, those policies can not be judged as clear winners in practice as they were later thought to be by Keynesian disciples. It was really "Orwellian Economics" (continuous war spending) that finally extracted the US from the depression in the late 30s and Japan somewhat earlier (the subject of my paper somewhat later in the seminar series). The Gold Standard would have been a restraint on war preparations in both countries, so it was not in the interests served by military adventures to retain it.

Another important point is that a public debate over policy issues can serve a coordination function when there is a clear winner that convinces most economic agents of the appropriateness of a given policy such that they make their decisions based on that policy and the belief in the policy's consequences -- of course, in order for this to achieve a genuine coordination, the policy must be consistent with reality and with expectations based on it. You wrote

> This is exactly a reason why we focus on the role of ideas. Suppose that there is some winning policy idea, or preoccupied idea in our terminology, that has successfully convinced most economic agents. As long as this conventional idea is consistent at least roughly with reality, preoccupation would do no harm. Rather, it would minimize a cost of social consent. A problem would occur when the conventional idea is inconsistent with reality in some fatal aspects. We think we are dealing with these cases.

You probably are, but it may be advisable to read *The Fatal Conceit* to be sure which is which. You may also find the following from Brad DeLong in the current *Foreign Affairs* an interesting characterization:

> Harry Johnson, in his superb but not entirely fair critique of Milton Friedman's Monetarists, said that in order to carry out an intellectual revolution in economics, one must propound a doctrine that has three qualities: it can be summarized in a single sentence, it provides the young with an excuse for ignoring the work of their elders, and it tells the young what they can do to further the revolution. John Maynard Keynes and Friedman both offered such doctrines. They said, respectively, that "aggregate demand determines supply" and that "inflation is always and everywhere a monetary

phenomenon"; they dismissed their predecessors as obsolete; and they set hundreds of young to the task of estimating consumption, investment, and money-demand functions.

Zane's support for a colleague

As WELL AS engaging newcomers to his circle in extended email debate, Zane was also keen to help young colleagues advance in their careers. In the following letter of support for Filip Palda's application for his school's research prize (which Palda did not win) we see Zane at his literary and analytical best. Taking the time to review a colleagues' life work in depth, to dwell upon it for some time, and then in a few pages to summarize it in a balanced and comprehensible manner. Here then is this one of a kind letter Zane could produce at will.

To the selection committee of ENAP: The following is to support Professor Filip Palda's application for the ENAP research prize. ENAP is a well-respected multi-disciplinary research institution where Professor Palda's many diverse research interests have found important expression. In a line allow me to summarize the character of Professor Palda's research: his research depends little on what has gone before, is deceptively simple in presentation, and serves others as a starting point for their researches. As such, Palda is an innovator and is responsible for important contributions to a number of fields in economics and in public choice. Allow me to outline what I believe to have been his major contributions.

Starting with this undergraduate dissertation from Queen's university, which was published when Palda was 22 years old in the journal *Public Choice*, and which has become widely quoted, Palda made his first name for himself as a founder of the industrial organization of campaign finance legislation. What this means, for the non-economist is that Palda formally modeled the effects on political competition of campaign finance laws. At the time of his analysis, competition was thought to mean simply how close an election race turned out to be. Palda argued instead that competition is determined by barriers to entry, and in a seminal piece in 1995 showed that margins of victory in election campaigns can be a poor indicator of competition.

Palda's empirical work in the field was seminal in showing that incumbents had a vested interest in imposing spending limits because the productivity of their campaign spending was lower than that of challengers. Perhaps his most innovative and technically masterful treatment of campaign finances came in his 2000 *Public Choice* article in which he demonstrated the completely novel proposition that it was not just what candidates spent that determined election outcomes but also where they got their money. Palda's contributions in this field also include two highly respected books, and his stature was confirmed when he was asked to contribute two survey articles on campaign spending and the related issue of interest group dynamics to the prestigious encyclopedia of Public Choice project. In addition, Dennis Mueller cites him in his comprehensive survey of Public Choice. As I understand he was also instrumental as an expert legal advisor in two Alberta court cases where his advice helped to defeat a federal law gagging spending by private groups during elections.

Related to but different from his research into campaign finances, Palda also attacked the very old problem of why people vote. It had been a Public Choice dogma that when an election race is close people are more likely to vote because they feel their vote could make a difference to the outcome of the election. The problem with earlier studies was that they were based on district-level data. This created a problem of simultaneity: was overall turnout a function of closeness or was closeness a function of turnout? Attempts to get around the ecological fallacies inherent when inferring micro-behaviour from macro-results were no more successful. Surveys asked people what their perceived closeness was. So was their decision to turn out a function of their perceived closeness or did people rationalize their voting decision by saying they perceived the race as close. What Palda and his colleague Matsusaka did in two powerful studies was to meld macro-measures of closeness with micro-surveys of Canadian elections. The macro closeness measure was thus objective. To the surprise and consternation of many who had made their livelihood supporting the turnout-closeness hypothesis Palda and Matsusaka found no effect of closeness on turnout (I must add in addition that their research was so rich in empirical detail that they were the first to investigate the effects of weather on turnout but relegated this result to an appendix). Their two papers on this topic are heavily quoted in economics and also to some degree in political science.

Palda's other main branch of research contributions belongs to the tax evasion literature, both theoretical and empirical. In 1998 he published the first of a string of articles which explored the survival of economic actors into whose fitness was coded a productive efficiency parameter and a parasitical parameter (such as the ability to evade taxes). His 1998 article is the first theoretical treatment of what Palda has coined as displacement deadweight loss (DDL). What made this article truly seminal was its combination of the invention of a new technique for analysis in economics, wedded to an original idea about human behaviour, all of which culminated in a cornucopia of results, some expected, some unexpected.

Palda's methodological innovation was to adapt an obscure graphical and mathematical method from statistics for the calculation of the distributions of functions of two random variables, to the modeling of supply and demand when supply is determined not just by cost but by evasive ability. I see this method as having important applications in labour economics, especially in the representation of the Roy model of profession selection. Palda used his totally novel method to see who would survive in a market where each producer had randomly drawn evasive and productive abilities. By comparing the costs of producers in a market without evasion to the costs of producers in a market with evasion he was able to calculate the DDL. Remarkably, his work also showed that tax revenues could be higher under tax evasion than without tax evasion (the interpretation being that tax evasion allows government to "price discriminate" among producers).

Palda extended his insights to the evasion of minimum wages in an article which I believe to the be the best theoretical work he has done. The piece is too complex to describe here, but let me say I believe it is quite ahead of anything being done in the field today. In a way, that is Palda's problem. I understand that he has been time and again rejected by the SSHRC. I attribute this to the fact that his research usually has no precedent, and to the fact that Palda generally prefers to work alone; a characteristic of researchers with a strong vision. I was gratified to learn that in the last two or three years Palda has received three substantial research grants (two from the prestigious Global Development Network of the World Bank). That goes to show the power of working in a team (he got the grants in collaboration with a colleague) and also of proposing slightly less original projects (he is getting money to do bread-and-butter surveys of tax evaders in transition countries).

But to continue, Palda has also published a piece in *Public Choice* where he melds his ideas on twin-talents to a game-theoretic framework in order to come up with a new type of rent-seeking cost. Up to that time only three forms of rent-seeking cost had been identified. Palda came up with the fourth. His work in this area continues and his working paper on the issue in which he deepens his techniques, is among the most downloaded of working papers in the international economics working paper archives on public finance.

Palda's other work on tax evasion deserves mention. This work is less theoretical, and two of his efforts in this field I find to be rather ordinary and unoriginal. But two others deserve special mention. One is his recent pieces with Jan Hanousek showing that people pay taxes not because they are afraid of being caught evading, but because they believe they are getting good quality government services. To date no one had really championed this hypothesis, and their article, though published only this year, is getting a lot of attention from researchers in this growing field. Their other piece which is of interest to me uses Markov chain analysis melded to surveys Palda and Hanousek have themselves devised, to develop a method for forecasting tax evasion five years out. This again is completely novel work and had no precedent in the field.

So much for Palda's two "big" areas of research. He has also made cameo appearances in a number of other sub-fields of economics. His *Kyklos* paper on political efficiency was the first to analyse and measure fiscal churning. In fact I think Palda may have invented the term. Churning happens when government taxes a person and then returns part or all of that tax back to him via a subsidy. Palda measured churning for Canada (an enormous feat of number crunching) and tried to alert the Public Choice field to this neglected aspect of political inefficiency. This work is only now, seven years later, starting to be noticed. Palda also was the first to analyse how a dictator reacts to foreign aid. It was in fact this work which first brought me into contact with Palda 14 years ago as I was assigned as the commentator on this piece at a conference of the European Public Choice society.

I may have missed some of Palda's other research, but I think I have covered the main points. I will briefly mention that Palda is one of those rare researchers who is not content to let others carry his results into the field of public policy, but that Palda has himself been an active popularizer and advocate of his work. Twice he acted as court expert to defeat a federal gag law on campaign spending by third parties. He also wrote a delightful, almost poetic book on the economics of Canadian cities and how public policy in Canadian cities should be conducted. He has edited books on transportation policy, interprovincial trade barriers, the stock market, and Quebec economic policy. In addition he was the architect of the methodology and computer programming used by the Fraser Institute throughout the 1990s for their calculations of the true tax burdens Canadians pay and this resulted in three books by him on this topic.

I suppose I could go on, because I am sure I have missed some points, but I believe this letter has reached a great enough length. I hope this helps the committee of ENAP on making an informed judgment in their research competition awards.

Zane Spindler, Full Professor
Simon Fraser University

CONTRIBUTORS 8

DOUGLAS ALLEN, THE Burnaby Mountain Professor of Economics, received his B.A.(hons) (1983) and M.A. (1984) from SFU, and his Ph.D. (1988) from the University of Washington where he studied under Professor Yoram Barzel. He was an assistant professor at Carleton University in Ottawa before moving to SFU in 1990. His field of study is the economics of transaction costs and property rights, and he has applied this methodology to understanding institutions like marriage and divorce, welfare, the church, farm organization, homesteading, and the military. His latest book *The Institutional Revolution* was recently published by the University of Chicago Press. Allen took his very first macroeconomics course with Zane in the fall of 1979 and received a B-, his all-time lowest economics mark. Although this low grade rescued him from a career in macro, later, on squash courts in the 1990s, Zane paid dearly for the error of his past grading ways.

BRIAN DOLLERY IS Professor of Economics and Director of the Centre for Local Government at the University of New England. He has written extensively on local government, especially on local government structure, finance and reform. Recent books include *Funding the Future* (2013), *Councils in Cooperation* (2012), *Local Government Reform: A Comparative Analysis of Advanced Anglo-American Countries* (2008), *The Theory and Practice of Local Government Reform*

(2008), *Reform and Leadership in the Public Sector* (2007) and *Australian Local Government Economics* (2006). Over the past two decades, Brian has worked with a large number of local councils across Australian, mostly on structural reform.

CEDRIC NATHAN EARNED a Ph.D. in Economics from Simon Fraser University, British Columbia, Canada, in 1974, following a Masters degree in Economics from the London School of Economics. He taught graduate and undergraduate courses in Macroeconomics and International Finance at various Canadian universities, before taking a full-time position in the Economics Department at the University of Cape Town, South Africa. In 1993, Nathan and Zane received the Donald Robertson Memorial prize for the most distinguished article in *Urban Studies*, where rent-seeking theory was applied to a new squatting phenomenon in South Africa. For many years (from the early 1990s), Cedric internationalized the South African economic transition debate - towards a universal franchise constitutional order - by organizing and participating in South Africa sessions at the Western Economic Association International annual conferences. These and other research are published in refereed journals. As a result, the Economics Department at the University of Cape Town benefited from visits by internationally renowned economists. Cedric retired from the University of Cape Town in 2007.

ASAHI NOGUCHI IS Professor of Economics at Senshu University in Kawasaki, Japan. He studied at the University of Tokyo. His research topics cover a variety of areas related to international economics, history of economic theory, and economic policy. He has written numerous Japanese books and published articles both in Japanese and English on these topics. Recent articles include "Shifting Domestic and International Perceptions of Japan's Economy," *Japanese Journal of Political Science*, Volume 13, Part 2, June 2012, "The State of Macroeconomics in View of the Global Economic Crisis," in *Keynesian Reflections: Effective Demand, Money, Finance, and Policies in the Crisis*, edited by Toshiaki Hirai, Maria Cristina Marcuzzo, and Perry Mehrling, Oxford University Press, 2013, and "Controversies Regarding Monetary Policy and Deflation in Japan from the 1990s to the early 2000s," in *The Development of Economics in Japan: From the Inter-war Period to the 2000s*, edited by Toichiro Asada, Routledge, 2014.

FILIP PALDA is professor of economics at the École nationale d'administration publique. He received his Ph.D. from the University of Chicago in 1989.

ROGER J. SANDILANDS is Emeritus Professor of Economics at the University of Strathclyde, Glasgow. A graduate of Strathclyde and Simon Fraser Universities, he has had a varied international teaching and research career that often overlapped with Zane Spindler's: in Canada, the UK, Colombia, Singapore, and Japan. He has also held visiting positions in Sweden, Peru and China. For several years he was Managing Editor of the *Journal of Economic Studies*. He wrote an intellectual biography of the distinguished New Dealer and FDR's White House adviser, Lauchlin Currie (Duke University Press, 1990), with whom both he and Zane had close links in Canada and Colombia. As president of the Scottish League for Land Value Taxation, he has been interested in Henry George and Ricardian rent theory that for many years pitted him against Zane's opposing interest in public choice theories of rent-seeking.

XAVIER DE VANSSAY is Professor of Economics at York University (Glendon College). He received his Ph.D. from Simon Fraser University, and joined Glendon's Economics Department in 1990. Since then, he has been a Visiting Professor at Sciences Po (Paris) and other universities. He has published scholarly articles on theoretical and empirical aspects of public policy issues as well as on international economics.

"PALDA OFFERS A *novel and interesting perspective on ideas familiar to economists but which are not widely shared. This perspective will surely broaden the understanding of the political economy in which we live.*" **James M. Buchanan, Nobel Prize economics, 1986**

IN PARETO'S REPUBLIC Palda argues that economists have discovered a system of "social accounting" without even knowing it. Supply and demand in private markets create a "Pareto-efficient" equilibrium in which no one can be made better off without hurting at least one person. Palda argues this form of social accounting keeps societies that subscribe to it cohesive and prosperous and that it dominates rival systems of social accounting such as Marxism and Utilitarianism. The book is also an excellent introduction to the Coasian analysis of property rights, public finance analysis of taxation and spending, and Public Choice theory.

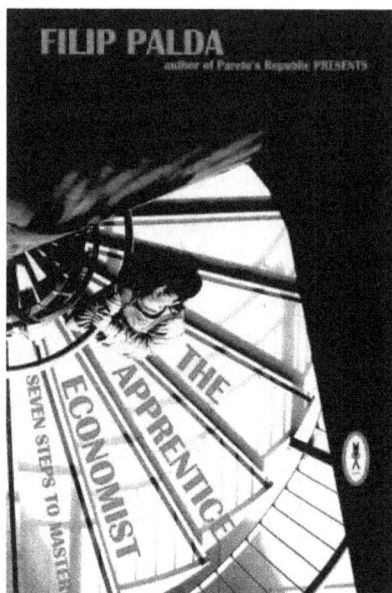

About Cooper-Wolfling

COOPER-WOLFLING IS A publisher of economics treatises and of portraits of contemporary economists. The goal is to provide books which are of interest to the general public but which may also be of use in the classroom. WWW.COOPWOLF.COM

Complimentary ebook copy

Email to **INFO@PARETOREPUBLIC.COM** for a complimentary ebook copy of Pareto's Republic and The Apprentice Economist. In your email supply the following complimentary book code in either the subject line or anywhere in the text: FREEPARAPP1099. Supply is limited to the first 100 requests.

www.ingramcontent.com/pod-product-compliance
Lightning Source LLC
Chambersburg PA
CBHW031958190326
41520CB00007B/290